STUDIES IN THE BRITISH ECONOMY

BANKS AND MARKETS

STUDIES IN THE BRITISH ECONOMY

General Editor: Derek Lee

1. Monopoly *by Derek Lee, Vivian Anthony and Allen Skuse*
2. Regional Planning and the Location of Industry *by Derek Lee*
3. Britain's Overseas Trade *by Vivian Anthony*
4. Government Intervention and Industrial Policy *by Allen Skuse*
5. The Trade Unions *by Hugh Williamson*
6. Control of the Economy *by Derek Lee*
7. Banks and Markets *by Vivian Anthony*
8. Advertising *by Eric Savage*
9. National Economic Planning *by Cedric Sandford*
10. National Income and Expenditure *by Samuel Hays*
11. The Structure of British Industry *by M. Dunn and P. Tranter*
12. The Engineering Industries *by Samuel Hays*
13. The Distributive Trades *by Frank Livesey*
14. British Population *by R. M. Williams*
15. The Chemicals and Allied Industries *by Samuel Hays*
16. The United Kingdom and the World Monetary System *by Brinley Davies*
17. Britain and the Developing Countries *by M. McQueen*
18. Pricing in Practice *by J. R. Davies and S. Hughes*
19. Resource Allocation and Cost Benefit Analysis *by R. Thomas*
20. Business Finance and the City *by Brinley Davies*
21. Britain and the EEC *by D. Lewis*
22. British Agriculture *by Brian Hill*
23. Investment in the British Economy *by J. R. Davies and S. Hughes*

STUDIES IN THE BRITISH ECONOMY

Banks and Markets

THIRD EDITION

by
Vivian S. Anthony
Headmaster, Colfe's School, London

HEINEMANN EDUCATIONAL BOOKS
LONDON

Heinemann Educational Books Ltd
22 Bedford Square, London WC1B 3HH
LONDON EDINBURGH MELBOURNE AUCKLAND
HONG KONG SINGAPORE KUALA LUMPUR NEW DELHI
IBADAN NAIROBI JOHANNESBURG
EXETER (NH) KINGSTON PORT OF SPAIN

First published 1972
Second Edition 1974
Reprinted 1975
Third Edition 1979

British Library C.I.P. Data

Anthony, Vivian Stanley
Banks and markets. – 3rd ed. –
(Studies in the British economy).
1. Banks and banking – Great Britain
I. Title II. Series
332.1'0941 HG2990

ISBN 0 435 84578 0

Set, printed and bound in Great Britain by
Fakenham Press Limited, Fakenham, Norfolk

PREFACE TO THE FIRST EDITION

Banks and Markets deals with the recent development in an area where changes have been considerable and of fundamental importance. A good understanding of the way in which Britain's monetary system works in the present day is only possible if the reader appreciates how the various institutions which make up the system are operating, and adapting themselves to current pressures.

In such a small book it has not been possible to deal with all the institutions of the system. A thorough treatment of the foreign exchange and commodity markets and of such important institutions as finance houses, building societies, and the stock exchange will have to await a later volume dealing with the markets for longer term money.

Where it seemed essential there has been some attempt to explain the theory which lies behind the operations and developments of the banks and markets but this is an essay in applied and descriptive economics and the reader would do well to familiarize himself with the basic theory from one of the standard texts. It is hoped that this book will help to show the relevance and meaning of the theory.

My wife has been most helpful in her encouragement and in reading the manuscript and typing parts of it. The Economics Method Group in the Department of Education at Leeds University have made some helpful comments on the diagrams.

V. S. Anthony
November 1971

PREFACE TO THE SECOND EDITION

The first edition of this book went to print soon after the Bank of England introduced the new arrangements for competition and credit control. While these may turn out to be changes more in name than in practice they are clearly of considerable significance. Parts of the book have been rewritten with these changes in mind. The revision of the final chapter has also been greatly aided by the work I have done with Derek Lee on his book in this series *Control of the Economy*. I am grateful to him for allowing me to reproduce some of the ideas in this book.

V. S. Anthony
1974

PREFACE TO THE THIRD EDITION

In preparing the new edition of this book, I have retained much of the earlier material so that students can fully understand the nature of the changes which have taken place in this decade. The tables have been updated, and the final chapter reviews the developments which have taken place since the last edition.

V. S. Anthony
1979

CONTENTS

INTRODUCTION		viii
CHAPTER 1	The Bank of England	1
CHAPTER 2	The Commercial Banks	27
CHAPTER 3	The Discount Market	58
CHAPTER 4	The Merchant Banks	76
CHAPTER 5	The London Gold Market	90
CHAPTER 6	Secondary Money Markets	99
CHAPTER 7	Government Policy	115
CHAPTER 8	Recent Developments in British Banking	132
	Bibliography	149
	Essay Questions	153
	Index	157

INTRODUCTION

The financial institutions of this country have in the past been shrouded in mystery. The shroud was partly the creation of the institutions who veiled their activities with great secrecy, and partly stemmed from the fact that even when the activities were explained people found them difficult to understand. The City of London where most of these institutions are centred has not always welcomed inquiries and publicity. Even in 1971 Sir Frederick Catherwood, the retiring Director-General of the National Economic Development Office, was moved to criticize the City for its failure to aid the creation of an economic development committee for financial services. 'The City,' he said, 'can contribute much more to the general economic debate.' The institutions of the City argued that such a committee would be simply duplicating work which is already done by other organizations in the City.

In the last decade or so much of the mystery has been lifted from the workings of these financial institutions. The report of the Radcliffe Committee on the Working of the Monetary System in 1959 did a great deal to further understanding of the way in which the institutions of the system worked. Since this report a great deal has been written about the various banks and markets which make up the system. The Prices and Incomes Board investigated bank charges. The Monopolies Commission reported on proposed bank mergers. The Select Committee on the Nationalized Industries looked at the Bank of England, and the Bank of England and other banks have invited in management consultants. It was a time ripe for inquiry with so much change and development under way.

The traditional use of monetary weapons has been subjected to intense scrutiny and criticism. The commercial banks have argued loudly how unfairly the weapons of credit restriction are directed. Other institutions are able to continue to increase their lending when a rigid ceiling is applied to bank advances. Monetary experts point out the fallacy of restricting credit by tightening the money markets when 'back-door lending' from the Bank of England by the discount houses lets the institutions of the market 'off the hook'. Others say that a policy of reducing the money supply by contracting the 'cash base' will be ineffective as long as government borrowing in the market continues to expand. We shall try to find out if there is substance in these criticisms.

The catalyst for changing the banks and markets has undoubtedly been growing competition, domestic and international. Whether the economic difficulties of the 1960s, rapidly rising running costs, the growth of new money markets, and other factors played a greater or a lesser part remains to be seen in later chapters, but it is certain that the need for the government to adopt severely restrictive credit control measures affected the growth rate of certain institutions in the market. That the balance of payments deficits had finally to be dealt with by devaluation, and that powerful inflationary pressures still remain, makes some bankers question if the sacrifice of the growth of these institutions has in the end been worthwhile. This conflict of interest is clearly recognized by the Bank of England. In a lecture given in December 1970 the Governor said '. . . monetary policy is conducted within a particular framework of institutions and markets. This framework provides opportunities, of course, but it also creates constraints. It is an important responsibility of the central bank to foster the growth and efficiency of the financial system as a whole; and its aims in these directions may from time to time, clash with the immediate goals of monetary policy.' Since 1971 banks and markets have been faced with the need to adapt to the changing conditions which have arisen from the new arrangements for competition and control of credit in the banking sector.

There will be few readers who are unaware that changes have been taking place in the banks and institutions of the money markets. A number of mergers have occurred among the joint stock banks and in the merchant bank world. The mergers and other link-ups between the banks have not only increased the scale of operations and brought out economies, but have also facilitated a diversification of operations, so that many more banks are active directly, or through their subsidiaries and associates, in all fields of banking, domestic and international. The new secondary money markets have provided these banks and other institutions with new, and profitable, lines of business – Euro-currencies, inter-bank loans, local authority loans and certificates of deposit – and there are very few banks which have not taken advantage of these.

There have been changes in the volume of business in the various traditional forms of paper dealt in the money markets. After years of dominance the relative importance of the Treasury bill declined rapidly, and the commercial bill has been in the ascendent. However, this has not been the traditional trade bill of exchange but the newer form, the finance bill. Many industrial and commercial borrowers have taken advantage of this form of short-term borrowing, and the discount houses, and other institutions of the short-term money market, have been quick to meet this demand. While the discount market has continued to deal in traditional forms of paper, it has also turned its attention to the new lines of business mentioned above.

The merchant banks have shown themselves to be among the most adaptable and go-ahead of Britain's financial institutions. They spread their net widely through a whole range of associates and subsidiaries at home and abroad. They have kept up many of their traditional lines of business and responded with suitable provision of services where these lines have expanded or altered. They have also been at the forefront of the development of new lines of business, particularly in international investment activities and the provision of other international financial services. They have expanded their new issuing business for domestic and foreign borrowers; they have developed through their experience of the foreign exchange market an intricate market in Euro-currency borrowing and such new forms of paper as negotiable certificates of deposit; and they have been very active in the field of company finance, attracting a great deal of attention through the part they play in company mergers. Four merchant banks dominate the London Gold Market, and the establishment of a two-tier system, with a free market for some gold has been a significant development which has required some adaptation on their part. How the market will cope with the dramatic price rise of 1973 remains to be seen.

These are but some of the banks and markets where significant changes have occurred in the last decade or so. There can be no doubt that such important institutions as Building Societies, Insurance Companies, Finance Houses, Investment and Unit Trusts, Savings Banks and other special finance agencies, which have assets in excess of £50,000 million, have a profound effect on the workings of the money market in this country. The markets for foreign exchange and for commodities are also very much part of the financial scene of the City of London. An all-embracing survey of banks and markets should contain a description of the activities of these institutions, but in such a small volume as this, we will have to content ourselves with a recognition of their important part in the monetary activities of institutions in this country.

1.
THE BANK OF ENGLAND

A time of inquiry and change

At a time when most financial institutions are undergoing change and development it is perhaps not surprising that the institution which is at the apex of the British financial system should have been the subject of a great deal of investigation and discussion. This scrutiny has been carried out not only by critics from outside the Bank – by a Royal Commission on the working of the monetary system (Radcliffe) in 1959, and by a Select Committee of the House of Commons in 1970 – but also from inside – by the authors of a series of informative articles appearing in the *Bank of England Quarterly Bulletin*, and by the McKinsey Management Consultants study. In October 1969 there was a conference on the operation of monetary policy in the ten years since the Radcliffe report. We have seen that the validity of monetary policy has been in debate, and with a great deal more information at their disposal critics have come to question other aspects of the affairs and the position of the Bank of England. The relationship between the government and the Bank, the Bank's charges and profits, the principle of public accountability as applied to the Bank, its position as 'representative of the City', and that of guardian of the good order of the financial system have all been subjected to scrutiny.

The Bank's position at the centre of the financial affairs of this nation has evolved gradually over almost three centuries since foundation in 1694, although the main developments towards its present position have occurred in the second half of its life. From the start it was closely involved in the business of lending to the government, but its monopoly of the issue of notes in England and Wales was not a feature until after the Bank Charter Act of 1844. The modern system of debt management based on the issue, buying and selling of Treasury bills and government bonds developed in the later nineteenth and early twentieth centuries, and its close involvement in the carrying out of government monetary policy and the intimate relationship with the Treasury is largely a twentieth century development fostered by the exigencies of wartime and the nationalization of the Bank in 1946. But even after the passing of the Act of Nationalization in 1946 and various Acts controlling the issue of notes and coins, the powers and responsibilities of the Bank of England in the present day are not based on statute so much as on an acceptance of these powers and responsibilities by the other financial institutions and on a recognition of the special semi-independent position of the Bank by the government. In Britain there is no general banking legislation defining the position of the Central Bank in relation to the other financial institutions and the government.

The present-day role of the Bank of England

Since its nationalization in 1946 the old distinction between the work which the Bank carried out for the government and the execution of its own affairs has not been a useful one. While it maintains a measure of independence from the government almost all its actions are influenced by the dictates of economic policy. The highly technical nature of the business of carrying out economic policy gives the Bank, which employs much of the expertise in this field, a powerful say in the discussions which precede policy decisions and an even more powerful say in its execution. But the position of the Governor of the Bank is essentially that of an adviser: the ultimate responsibility is with the Treasury. We will return to the relationship between the Bank and the Treasury later for the Bank performs many of its functions on behalf of the Treasury, and usually stands between the City and the Treasury. The need for expertise is evident in the Bank's dealings with the monetary authorities of other countries, and clearly these operations are bound up with the government's external economic policy. Here the objects of the government and the Bank are to produce conditions favourable to British trading interests and to secure equilibrium in the balance of payments. Deficit on the balance of payments means that foreign currency is leaving the country, and it is to control this outflow that the Bank of England operates exchange control.

Exchange control

The 1947 Exchange Control Act empowers the Treasury to exercise control over the movement abroad of gold, currency, and securities, and the import, export, transfer and settlement of property. The Bank, acting on behalf of the Treasury, requires transactors to ask for consent for such business. Certain banks, depositories and travel agents are authorized by the Bank of England to deal with many of these applications for which consent would almost automatically be granted, and to execute payments and other transactions on their own account and on behalf of their clients. Most of the payments associated with visible trade and many of the invisible items suffer little control but the larger capital items are subjected to much greater scrutiny. In 1971 there was an easing in restrictions on the amount of foreign exchange which travellers and tourists could take with them, and some reduction in the premium which British residents buying property abroad have to pay. The surpluses on the balance of payments 1969–71 soon changed to deficits 1972–74 and this cycle continued throughout the decade, but the important role of the Bank of England has in no way been diminished.

Exchange Equalization Account

A further external role of the Bank is the management of the Exchange Equalization Account established in 1932 to prevent undue fluctuations in the exchange value of the currency. Such fluctuations are not in the interests of traders and can produce disturbing movements of short-term funds between countries. In 1946 the powers of the E.E.A. were extended to cover the maintenance of adequate reserves of gold and foreign currencies. The reserves are kept by the E.E.A. at the Bank of England, and it lends to the Exchequer the proceeds of the sales of gold or foreign currencies, while it draws the sterling it requires from the Consolidated Fund, and holds its assets in the form of Treasury Bills. It operates in the Spot and Forward markets in accordance with government policy. When the exchange rate is fixed the Spot (present) rate is not allowed to vary beyond fixed limits. After the devaluation in 1967 these rates were £1 = $2·38 to £1 = $2·42. If the exchange value is in danger of falling below the lower limit, the E.E.A. uses its foreign currency reserves to buy sterling abroad, in this way pushing up exchange value of sterling. In the event of the rate for the pound pushing at the upper limit the E.E.A. would use pounds to buy foreign currencies building up Britain's reserves, which are usually held in U.S. dollars and gold. The international currency situation, never noted for its stability, has in the 1970s become remarkably unstable. As a result several countries, Britain among them, decided to float their exchange rate. Even though the currency crises were more associated with the dollar than with sterling the E.E.A. was very active in this period for even when the pound is floating efforts have to be made to prevent damaging short term fluctuations. Most of its activity was however in support of the dollar. There was pressure on the U.K. to join with its Common Market partners in a unified float against the dollar but it proved impossible to achieve agreement on the concept of unlimited support to make the system proof against major short-term capital flows. The task of safeguarding the nation's reserves gives the Bank an interest in the London Gold Market. Until recently the Bank acted as agent for the South African authorities selling the greatest part of the world's newly mined gold, but this is described in another chapter.

Relations with other central banks and international institutions
The Bank manages not only Britain's reserves but also those of the whole sterling area. The monetary authorities of the countries in the sterling area are in close and regular contact with the Bank, which buys and sells gold and foreign currencies on their behalf. It also manages their sterling holdings, usually investing them in Treasury bills, and advises them on the issue of stock on the London market when they are raising funds for their own governments. The movement of capital between countries in the sterling area is subject to much less restriction than the movement of funds out of the area.

As the central banker for the sterling area the Bank is inevitably in close contact with the central banks of non-sterling area countries, particularly U.S.A., Canada, and the countries of Western Europe. At times of crisis for sterling, which have not been uncommon since the last war, the Bank has played a major part in organizing support for the currency. The negotiation of standby loans from the I.M.F. has also been carried out by Bank officials. In 1969–70 Bank officials visited eighty-nine countries and received visits from 104 countries' officials. The Bank has frequent business with the I.M.F. and B.I.S., and other international financial institutions with whom it represents Britain's interests, and those of the sterling area. A close relationship has developed with the central banks of other leading industrial nations (the Bankers' Club) and these international institutions so that now there is a regular and intimate exchange of views and information. The I.M.F. gives its findings on the prospects for the British economy and what must be done to improve the position.

The domestic role
While the overseas work of the Bank is concerned with transfers between sterling and other currencies, the Bank's work at home deals with transfers of sterling between the public and private sectors, or,

as the Radcliffe reports puts it: putting sterling in or taking it out of the system. The object of the government's economic policy, and the Bank's management of the nation's money as part of that policy, is to create an economic environment which is favourable to the growth of the national income at an acceptable rate, but unfavourable to rising prices and unemployment. The achievement of this dynamic equilibrium depends on there being just enough money in the system to buy all the goods and services produced by a fully employed community (say, no more than 2 per cent unemployed) at the current level of prices. In its execution of government policy with these ends in view the Bank has no powers laid down by law and no official list of financial institutions which come under its control. The Bank relies largely on 'moral suasion' to impose quantitative and qualitative controls on the lending of financial institutions. Its sanctions derive from the recognition of its position and the value of its support and facilities by these institutions, who are therefore reluctant to incur its displeasure. We will return to the other weapons available to the Bank later in the chapter.

An examination of the balance sheet of the Bank of England gives a picture of the role which the Bank plays in this country.

BALANCE SHEET OF BANK OF ENGLAND
ON 15TH NOVEMBER 1978

Issue Department

LIABILITIES	£ million	ASSETS	£ million
Notes in Circulation	8,595	Government Securities	7,559
Notes in Banking Department	5	Other securities	1,041
	8,600		8,600

Banking Department

LIABILITIES		ASSETS	
Public Deposits	23	Government Securities	1,832
Special Deposits	1,105	Advances and other Accts	209
Bankers Deposits	417	Premises, Equipment and other Securities	169
Reserves and other Accts	656	Notes and Coin	5
Total	2,215	Total	2,215

Since the 1844 Bank Charter Act laid down provisions for the Bank to have a monopoly of note issue in England and Wales, the Bank has been required to present its balance sheet under the two separate headings which correspond to the two departments of the Bank, the Issue Department and the Banking Department, even though this has little significance for the way in which the Bank works in the present day.

The Issue Department

The liabilities of the Issue Department consist entirely of Bank of England notes, of which the greater part are in circulation with the general public, and the remainder held in the Banking Department. No other notes circulate with legal tender in England and Wales but the Scottish and Irish Banks are allowed to issue their notes to certain maximum amounts, and they circulate in those countries alongside Bank of England notes. The Currency and Bank Notes Act of 1954 permitted a fiduciary issue (note issue not secured by gold but by government securities) of £1,575 million. The Fiduciary Note Issue (Extension of Period) Order is laid before Parliament every two years by the Treasury on the instigation of the Bank to obtain the permission of Parliament for an extension of the note issue above the statutory limit. The fiduciary issue now amounts to more than £3,500 million. While some control of the note issue is clearly needed (governments have been known to print more paper as a way of meeting their debts), it is of secondary importance to the control of other types of money – bank deposits, H.P., etc. The Bank's main concern is to provide just enough notes to meet conveniently the needs of the customers of the commercial banks, and to do this as cheaply as possible. There has been a good deal of discussion of the cost of providing this facility in the last few years. The British public has in the past proved unwilling to use notes that have been in circulation for some time and have become dirty. So notes were being exchanged for clean ones so frequently that the demand for new notes from the Issue Department was increasing rapidly and the cost of the currency was becoming a cause for concern. In 1969 1,800 million notes were printed at a cost of £5 million, which shows an increase of 5 per cent p.a. in recent years. There have to be enough notes to meet demand at the peak times of Christmas, Easter and August. The notes are issued to the banks through the branches of the Bank of England and from the Head office. The changeover to decimal currency has given the Bank and the Treasury an opportunity to restructure the currency. As a result the ten shilling note was replaced by a coin as part of a redesigned coinage, and a new denomination note at £10 was introduced. Efforts are being made to encourage people to use notes of higher denominations. £5 notes already account for more than half the total value of all notes.

The National Loans Act of 1968 provides for the profits arising from the assets held by the Bank to secure the note issue to be paid into a National Loans Fund. Previously the profits had been paid to the Treasury and then into the Exchange Equalization Account. The assets of the Issue Department are the various kinds of Government debt – bonds and Treasury bills – which it holds, and the profits are what remains after the costs of printing, holding and distributing new notes and destroying old notes has been covered. They amounted to some £100 million in 1969–70. It can be seen that gold no longer plays a significant part in securing the nation's note issue. When an increase in the number and value of notes is sanctioned this is secured nowadays by the Bank holding an increased value of government securities. The Bank's promise to pay is thus secured by the government's promise to pay, and it is on the note-users' confidence in this promise that the whole practice of a fiduciary issue rests. This confidence has allowed an increase in the note issue from less than £500 million in 1939, to £1,500 million in 1953, to £2,500 million in 1964, and to more than £9,000 million in 1979.

The Banking Department

The first two items on the assets side of the balance sheet of the Banking Department have little significance since nationalization. Capital represents the investment of the proprietors of the Bank for which they were given government stock as compensation on nationalization. Rest is the reserve fund of the Bank, but at £3·9 million out of a total liability of almost £600 million it can do little more than provide for contingencies. Yet it is important that the Bank has, and is believed to have, 'fully adequate financial resources to fulfil all the functions it is called upon to undertake' (Select Committee).[1] Furthermore, it must not be 'inhibited in its choice of

---

[1] Select Committee here stands for 'The Report of the Select Committee on Nationalized Industries'. The examination was carried out by Sub-Committee B under the chairmanship of Colonel C. G. Lancaster, which was appointed in February 1969 and reported on 28 May 1970.

policies by fears that the costs will undermine, or be thought to undermine, its financial stability' (Select Committee). The Bank in practice finances its activities from the proceeds of the investment of the Bankers' Deposits, Special Deposits and Public Deposits (which are usually very small) in government securities, which yields 67 per cent of its income, 25 per cent coming from Proprietors funds, and 8 per cent from agencies. For the purpose of public confidence it is perhaps a good thing that the Bank emerges from the exercise of these activities with a profit, but the Select Committee was anxious to determine what use was made of this profit: a matter we will return to later.

Relationship with the government

It is clear from the balance sheet that the main customers of the Bank are the government and the clearing banks. Of the Bank's relationship with the government the Radcliffe Report says, it 'is the historical foundation of its pre-eminence in the City of London, and . . . the concept of the Bank as being first and foremost the government's banker still deeply colours the Bank's understanding of its own responsibilities and duties'. In the first place it holds the central accounts of the government – Public Deposits. This includes the Exchequer, National Loans Fund, National Debt Commissioners and Dividend Accounts and a number of subsidiary accounts. All normal payments by the various departments of the government and their receipts go through the Bank of England. If any of these departments find themselves temporarily out of funds the Bank gives overnight assistance in the form of Ways and Means Advances. All the various kinds of borrowing done by the government make up the National Debt, and this is managed for the government by the Bank of England.

The management of the National Debt

The Bank is responsible for the issue of all Treasury bills and government bonds, and also for buying back the bills and bonds as they reach maturity, or before that date, for redemption is gradual. It keeps a register of holders of all these securities and arranges payments of dividends and records transfers. There are some 2½ million accounts and almost 200 securities with a value of £22,000 million. In 1969–70 there were 750,000 transfers. It arranges through the Government Broker for the buying or selling of existing securities to influence the market as part of *Open Market Operations*[1] using the assets of the Issue Department. (The Government Broker is the senior partner of Messrs Mullens & Co.) The Bank also arranges the issue and manages the securities of the Nationalized Industries, some of the Commonwealth countries, Local Authorities and Public Boards. The value of Local Authority Bills now exceeds £75 million. It also marshalls the queue of borrowers in the new issue market. A Bank memorandum summarises the two facets of debt management: 'decisions by the Treasury, with the Bank's advice, on the issue, redemption or conversion of securities; and open market operations by the Bank to ensure the successful issue of new securities . . . and redemption of old securities'. The Bank's operations are continuous with gradual redemption and issue merged into daily operations, so that it is only the net balance of sales and securities which is significant in affecting the money market. The Bank has a number of aims in its debt policy and these are not always consistent. For instance the aim of keeping down interest rates so that the government can obtain its *funds as cheaply as possible* and so that the problems of future debt management are not increased is not consistent with a policy of *credit restraint where money has to be kept tight* so that inflationary tendencies in the economy can be controlled. The Bank is also influenced in its interest rate policy by the desire *to maintain the gold and foreign exchange reserves* of the country. It moves the rates up to attract short term capital from abroad, or to counter movements of capital away from this country. The Bank aims to *produce an orderly market for government securities* and so works to iron out unevenness in the market. The Bank must see to it that *the government always obtains its borrowing requirement*, but the considerable increase in this requirement, and in that for the public sector as a whole, increases the problem of controlling the money supply, and raises the question of whether the public sector is taking too large a share of the national wealth. Domestic investors other than the clearing banks and discount houses bought almost £900 million of government securities in 1969–70. We will examine other trends in debt management later in this chapter.

---

[1] The items in italics can be seen as the main aims of the Bank's debt policy.

Relationship with the clearing banks

The Bank both acts as banker to the clearing banks and exercises control over their activities in the execution of the government's monetary policy. This is thought by some to be a conflicting role on certain occasions. The Bank has come to represent the interests of the City with the Treasury but also to enforce Treasury policy which might be restraining the activities of these City institutions. The clearing banks all hold their cash reserves at the Bank. This is the item Bankers' Deposits in the balance sheet, and it is through this holding that the Bank exercises much of its control. The banks value the facility, which enables them to draw cash (notes) to meet customers' requirements, or transfer money (between accounts at the Bank) in settlement of debts with other banks, and are reluctant to do anything which might result in a withdrawal of this facility. The Bank of England is not obliged to maintain these accounts, and the clearing banks would suffer considerable cost and inconvenience, as well as loss of status, if the accounts were closed.

In practice the Bank of England does not have to resort to sanctions in its dealings with the clearing banks, although there was in 1971 a reduction in the rate of interest paid on Special Deposits as a reminder that the Bank expects its directives to be followed. The Bank can affect the power of the banks to create money by actions designed to reduce the eligible reserve assets, which has replaced the liquid assets ratio. From 1946 to 1971 it was a banking convention that the banks kept 8 per cent of their assets in the form of cash, part of which was held in the tills of the banks and the remainder held in their accounts at the Bank of England. Since September 1971 the requirement has been for the banks to hold $1\frac{1}{2}$ per cent in the form of cash, but till-money is no longer acceptable for this ratio. However the Bank of England had for some time found *the liquidity ratio* a more effective check on credit creation by the banks than *the cash ratio*. Liquid assets are those which a bank can quickly and easily convert into cash, which is a form of money generally acceptable as a means of settling its debts. Until the new arrangements all treasury bills, commercial bills, money at call and, of course, cash were included in the liquid assets, which had to be maintained in ratio to the total deposits of the clearing banks at a minimum of 28 per cent. If the liquid assets fell below this, or the cash below the cash ratio the banks were expected to take steps to sell some of their investments or call in some of their advances to restore the ratio. Under the new arrangements the concept of liquid assets has been replaced by that of eligible reserve assets, which are defined rather more narrowly than liquid assets (see p. 124). However the clearing banks must nowadays maintain a minimum ratio of only $12\frac{1}{2}$ per cent though this is against eligible liabilities, a rather more widely defined concept than total deposits (again see p. 124). There is however little basic change in the fundamental methods of controlling the banks' powers to create credit by operating on their liquidity (reserve assets) position.

Open market operations

The Bank of England can affect the banks' reserve assets position by buying or selling government securities. When it sells the banks, or their customers, are the buyers and this reduces the banks' deposits at the Bank of England as they have to use their cash. They must then take action to restore their cash ratio. A rise in the government's balances while the Bank of England's total assets (and therefore total liabilities) remain the same implies a fall in Bankers' Deposits (Sayers). So the Bank operates by influencing inflows and outflows of cash. The Bank frequently carries out *open market operations* (buying or selling government securities) to stabilize the fluctuating conditions of the market. On these occasions the Bank is acting neutrally, and actions to affect reserve assets usually work through the weekly tender of Treasury bills. The banks can almost always restore their reserve assets position by calling in loans from the discount houses, and if the latter are pressed for funds they can, in the last resort, and at a price, borrow from the Bank of England. Thus while the Bank of England may be operating a squeeze on the money market it will always, through the discount market, allow the market to discharge its debt obligations but profit margins will dwindle or even disappear until new rates of interest prevail in the market. 'The perfection attained in the English system is due primarily to the many decades through which the Bank of England has unreservedly accepted its obligations to lend freely in time of crisis, but it has also been helped by the unique structure of the discount market as a buffer between the central bank and the commercial banks'.[1] We return to this function of the Bank later. (See *Lender of Last Resort*, p. 14.) The Bank also makes available to the Clearing and Scottish Banks refinance facilities for export and shipbuilding credits. The effectiveness of open market operations depends on the

[1] Sayers R. S., *Modern Banking*.

margin which clearing banks keep over and above minimum cash and reserve asset requirements. When the margin is large the banks have a buffer against such operations.

Bank of England directives

When government policy requires it, the Bank of England, after discussions with the Treasury, issues directives to the clearing banks on how they are expected to cooperate to further the economic objectives. For example, on 19 November 1967 new measures of credit restrictions were announced to the banks. 'Severe but very selective restrictions will need to be placed on bank lending in sterling to the private sector and to borrowers abroad. It is essential that credit for the finance and promotion of exports should be free of all restriction.'[2] The notice goes on to specify ways in which lending should be curtailed, and directs that lending should be held down in aggregate to the then current level. Later directives required the banks to reduce their deposits to 98 per cent of that level. That the Bank of England has some sympathy with the difficulties of banks when such directives are issued is clear from the final paragraph of the November 1967 directive. 'The authorities recognize the difficulties that the banks may encounter in seeking to give effect to the guidance now given. The Bank of England will therefore be inviting all the main banking groups to regular and frequent discussions with the Bank, so that progress may be better examined and difficulties more easily surmounted.' In July 1970 the banks were sternly reminded not to take advantage of some easing of monetary restrictions to increase their deposits too rapidly (only 5 per cent). These directives do not have the power of law, but as we have already seen the banks are most unlikely to defy them. The directives do not specify a curtailment of the business of any particular bank or any particular customer, but only the whole or a class of business. A directive to National Westminster to restrict lending to the Imperial Chemical Industries would be considered most improper. There is, says Professor A. D. Bain's memorandum to the Select Committee, 'a great reluctance to interfere in the business relationship between *individual* financial institutions and individual customers'. With the new arrangements of September 1971 the Bank announced that directives would be concerned with qualitative rather than quantitative controls, and this was demonstrated in 1972 with the directive that lending to property speculators should be discouraged.

---

[2] *Bank of England Quarterly Bulletin* December 1967.

Special Deposits

While the banks do not defy these directives they have on occasions been tardy in carrying them out. It was the desire of the Bank of England not to overwork the *moral suasion* of the banks that led to the announcement of Special Deposits in 1958. The banks were called to hold additional balances above the 1·5 per cent cash ratio. When Special Deposits are called the Bank of England opens a special account for the clearing banks and debits their normal account (i.e. bankers' deposits). These assets do not count as part of the reserve assets ratio. The money is lent to the government so that its borrowing requirement is reduced. The banks receive on the deposits interest approximately equal to the average Treasury bill rate for the preceding week. The effect though is to transfer part of each banks assets out of the items eligible as reserve assets. The weapon was first used in 1960 but was not immediately successful. The banks had, at that time, a high level of investments in government securities which they sold off to restore their liquidity ratio. (This was, of course, reduced when 2 per cent of their cash was paid into the Special Deposit Account.) So the desired cut back in bank advances was not affected. The later use of the weapon has been more effective for in 1961 the banks had a smaller buffer of investments, but for most of the decade Special Deposits remained as a threatening gesture to persuade the banks to comply with the directives. In 1969 the authorities, dissatisfied with the efforts of the banks to comply with a directive, reduced the rate of interest on Special Deposits until such time as the banks brought their lending into line with the directed requirement. Special Deposits were increased to 2½ per cent of each bank's deposits in May 1970, and repaid in the last quarter of 1971, when the new arrangements were announced. However that there was no intention of abolishing Special Deposits soon became clear when late in 1972 the authorities called in 3 per cent Special Deposits. The idea of differential Special Deposits distinguishing between domestic and overseas assets was announced in March 1973.

Lender of last resort

The Bank of England has a considerable influence over the supply of funds in the money market and over the rates of interest which prevail there. When the Bank wishes to restrict the supply of funds and drive the interest rates up to discourage borrowers it can soak up the funds by selling more Treasury bills, and if there are no payments from the public sector to offset the transfer of funds from the private sector (involved in buying Treasury bills) then the banks, finding a fall in their cash position, call in their day to day loans from the discount houses. The houses are unlikely to be able to find funds to balance their books at the end of the day and they will be forced into the Bank as *lender of last resort*. This is the Bank of England's way of giving help to the market, but it will determine the rates at which lending will take place. This rate was until 1972 known as Bank rate and is now known as the minimum lending rate. In the past Bank rate could be raised when the Bank wanted to push up interest rates in the market. Nowadays the rate is fixed by a formula relating it to the Treasury bill rate. However the Bank retains its right to push up its minimum lending rate independent of the Treasury bill rate if it wishes to indicate a change in its monetary policy. The discount houses who rely on a margin between the rate at which they borrow and the rate which they receive for discounting bills, are forced to push up the rate at which they tender for the weekly issue of Treasury bills. The clearing banks, who traditionally do not buy the bills from the discount houses until at least a week has elapsed, find when the time comes that a higher rate has been established in the market, and they in turn raise their rates for lending in the market. The Bank of England has traditionally maintained an 'Open Back Door' by lending either by rediscounting eligible bills, which means buying back Treasury bills which have not run their full course to maturity, or simply by lending funds to the Discount Houses against the security of 'eligible' bills. Eligible bills include all Treasury bills and those Commercial bills that bear the acceptance signature of one of the acceptance houses recognized by the Bank, and held by one of the recognized discount houses. The Bank of England indicated at the time when the ending of Bank rate was announced that the money markets could no longer rely on open back door lending. The Bank reserved the right to limit such lending and to narrow the definition of 'eligibility'. Last resort loans are usually lent for seven days and at a penal rate.

Relationship with the Discount and Accepting Houses

The relationship between the Bank and the Accepting Houses has for long been a close one and since the new arrangements this relationship has been put on a more formal footing. Like the clearing banks they are required to maintain a reserve assets ratio and to keep $1\frac{1}{2}$ per cent of their assets in cash at the Bank of England. The accepting houses are represented in their dealings with the Bank by the Chairman of the Accepting Houses Committee. The quality of the bills they accept is checked and the Bank issues directives to them and calls Special Deposits from them. Contacts between the Bank and the discount houses have been even closer for all the members of the London Discount Market Association have Loan Accounts at the Bank and on its special relationship over last resort lending 'the functioning of the monetary system as we know it depends', as the Radcliffe report commented. Discount Houses were at first required to maintain a 50 per cent ratio of assets in the form of public sector lending, but in July 1973 this requirement was replaced by the 'twenty-times multiplied'.

Bank rate

The 1946 Nationalisation Act provided for the Bank of England to influence interest rates more directly by declaring a change in Bank rate after consultation with the Treasury when economic circumstances made it desirable. Since 1946 this Bank rate, which was defined as the minimum rate at which the Bank would lend to the money market, played a central part in monetary policy, and it was widely accepted in the money markets as the indicator of a change in interest rates. The rates which clearing banks charged their customers was geared to Bank rate, usually 2 per cent above. A rise in Bank rate which brought about a rise in the whole complex of other interest rates was therefore expected to discourage borrowing. It was a further objective of the Bank to match the needs of investors and the funds which savers are prepared to lend at a level which is acceptable in terms of national economic goals.

In October 1972 Bank rate was replaced by a 'minimum lending rate'. This was the culmination of a long period of criticism of the weapon and doubts about its effectiveness, coinciding as it did with a new approach to competition and credit control in the banking system. The banks had already been freed from their cartel arrangements linking lending and borrowing rates to Bank rate. Under the new arrangements instead of other rates changing with Bank rate the 'minimum lending rate' was to follow changes in the Treasury bill rate with the proviso that the Bank could announce unilateral changes in the rate when it wished to indicate a change of monetary policy. In November 1978 the rate was raised from 10 to 12½ per cent as part of a counter inflation package.

Funding

There is a further way in which the Bank can affect the liquidity of the banking system and thereby influence the economy and that is by a process known as *funding*, which is the conversion of short-term into longer term securities. This is part of the Bank's debt management activities. By issuing fewer Treasury bills or buying them up from the market and replacing them with a larger issue of government bonds or selling them on the market at a favourable rate, the Bank can bring about a change in the structure of the Clearing Banks' assets, increasing 'investments' and reducing the reserve assets. To restore their reserve assets ratio the banks have to cut down on their advances. Private borrowers then find it more difficult to obtain funds. As with all open market operations by the Bank the process works in reverse if the policy is to stimulate the economy by making money easier. In recent years the proportion of government debt held in the form of Treasury bills has declined. In 1969–70 the total of Treasury Bills fell by over £1,000 million, and in the previous year by more than £3,000 million, and between 1970 and 1978 the increase in the Treasury Bill issue was a small one.

Private customers

The Bank of England has a small private banking business. It allows its employees to open accounts, and certain public companies and individuals of particular standing who have close associations with the Bank are also allowed accounts. In recent times the Bank has tended to be easier in allowing new accounts to be opened for it believes that this private business has the merit of giving the Bank first hand experience of some of the practical aspects of day-to-day commercial banking. (*B.E.Q.B.* March 1969).

The departments of the Bank

The table below illustrates how all these various functions are divided among the departments of the Bank.

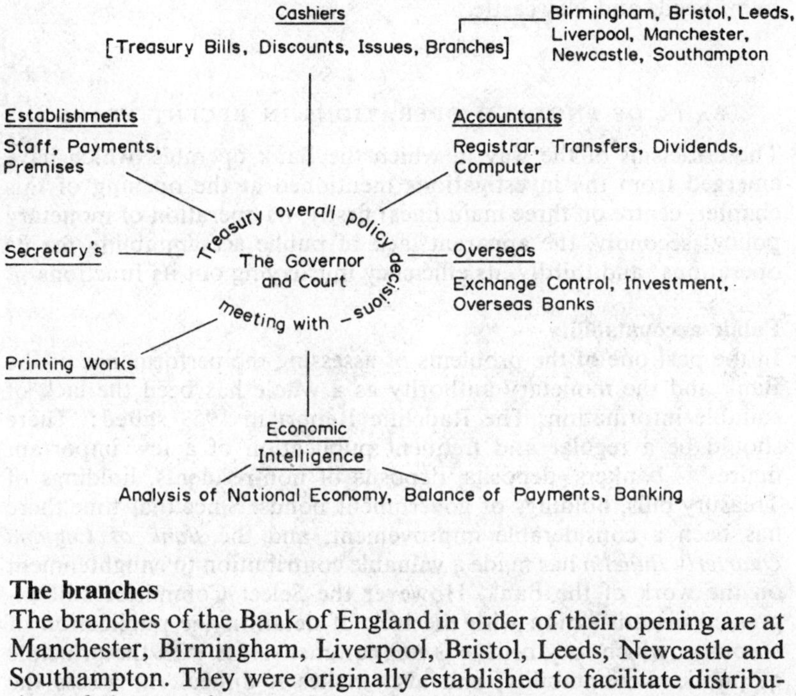

The branches

The branches of the Bank of England in order of their opening are at Manchester, Birmingham, Liverpool, Bristol, Leeds, Newcastle and Southampton. They were originally established to facilitate distribution of the note issue, a function which they continue to operate. They have a small number of private accounts and handle some of the receipts and payments of government accounts, particularly of the Customs and Excise and the Inland Revenue. More than half of the accounts maintained at the branches are government accounts. They deal with a wide range of applications for foreign exchange, and maintain close liaison with regional commodity markets. The clearing banks also keep accounts at the Bank of England branches. The officers of the branch banks are expected to keep their 'fingers on the pulse' of industry, and commerce in the regions. They report back to Head Office and attempt to give colour to government reports and statistics. This close personal contact with businessmen in the regions is believed to give a clearer picture of what is actually going on than the returns from the businesses to government departments, though this is not an opinion shared by the government departments. This side of the Bank's business has been increasing of late, and new premises are under construction at Manchester, Birmingham, Leeds and Newcastle.

BANK OF ENGLAND OPERATIONS IN RECENT YEARS

The criticisms of the way in which the Bank operates, which have emerged from the investigations mentioned at the opening of this chapter, centre on three main lines: firstly, its operation of monetary policy; secondly, the apparent lack of public accountability for its operations; and thirdly, its efficiency in carrying out its functions.

Public accountability

In the past one of the problems of assessing the performance of the Bank and the monetary authority as a whole has been the lack of suitable information. The Radcliffe Report in 1959 stated: 'There should be a regular and frequent publication of a few important figures' – bankers' deposits, deposits of non-residents, holdings of Treasury bills, holdings of government bonds. Since that time there has been a considerable improvement, and the *Bank of England Quarterly Bulletin* has made a valuable contribution to enlightenment on the work of the Bank. However the Select Committee still expressed dissatisfaction with the lack of detail in the publication of accounts, which they believe is not commensurate with the principle of public accountability, and also makes it difficult to assess the efficiency of the Bank's operations. The Bank argues that certain information cannot be made generally available because of the delicate nature of some of the activities of the Bank, particularly in the foreign exchange market, and where confidence in sterling could be affected. They would also regret any restriction imposed by the need to publish information on their 'doing good by stealth'. There have been occasions in the past when the Bank has helped out City financial institutions which have found themselves in serious, but temporary, difficulties which could have proved ruinous. The need to publicise these activities would clearly be a serious hindrance, and might make them impossible. The Bank is preparing to publish the accounts as part of the Annual Report in the future. The Bank clearly has a great deal more independence in these matters and over the question of the allocation of profits than other nationalized concerns, and the Select Committee was anxious to establish which of the Bank's independent activities were essential to the proper execution of its duties, and which were a mere continuation of traditions which in the name of public accountability should not continue.

Profits and efficiency

There is no legal provision for the payment of the profits that remain after suitable payments into the Bank's reserves. They do not *have* to be paid to the government. The Select Committee argue that since the Bank's profits arise largely from governmental actions, the Bank, besides making *economic charges* for its services to *all* customers including the government, should surrender its profits (except for reserves provision and working capital) to the government. They do not accept, as for other nationalized industries, that it is good for employee morale for profits to be retained for the use of the institution. In practice the profits of the Banking Department are used to make a half-yearly payment in lieu of dividend of £873,180 to the Treasury, and to allow the benefit to the Treasury of greatly reduced charges for the services it provides the government. The cost of Exchange Control is almost £2 million per annum, but the charge for these services has been only £50,000 since 1966. For the operation of the Exchange Equalization Account, which cost approximately £⅓ million 1967–68, the Bank makes no charge to the government. The scale of fees for the management of Stocks and Bond Issues have remained unchanged for more than twenty-five years, and now cover a small proportion of the costs of the work. The profits paid into the National Loans Fund as a result of the bond holding of the Issue Department now amount to approximately £2 million per annum. The Bank's investment also helps to pay for the statistical and information services and general banking services. It is clear that returns from the investment of Bankers' balances are being used to subsidize services to the government and others. In almost all cases of services provided by the Bank for the government there is either a nominal charge, a substantially reduced charge or no charge at all. The Select Committee criticized the lack of Treasury control over the internal investment policy of the Bank. They were not convinced by the Bank's argument for expenditure on branch bank buildings which had been financed out of investment income. They also pointed out that because of the nature of its activities and the derivation of its income it was difficult to assess the efficiency of the Bank. Clearly profits are not a true guide to its efficiency. But the Bank has a high reputation for the way it carries out its activities and there was no clear evidence that this was not deserved.

THE OPERATION OF MONETARY POLICY

The Bank has the dual responsibility of guarding the good order of the financial system, and carrying out the government's monetary policy. This responsibility has had to be carried out at a time when changes in financial institutions and markets have made it necessary for the Bank to adopt new measures to make its operations effective.

The declining share of the clearing banks in the total money supply
In 1960, the London clearing banks' deposits accounted for some 85 per cent of total sterling deposits, but the growth of other financial institutions had reduced their share to 70 per cent by 1970 even though the total value of their deposits had almost doubled. In June 1970 the clearing banks total of current and deposit accounts (including $ and £ certificates of deposit) amounted to £11,811 million out of the total accounts for the U.K. banking sector as a whole of £29,594 million. In April 1973 the London clearing banks accounted for £17,932 million out of a total of £73,067 million. The striking decline in their share of the market is illustrated by comparing these figures with those for 1963 when the deposit banks had accounts worth £8,445 million out of a total of £11,422 million. There has recently been a remarkable rise in the accounts of the accepting houses, overseas banks and other banks which have increased from £10,349 million in December 1968 to 17,577 million in June 1970, and by April 1973 amounted to more than £55,000 million, largely due to the enormous expansion of the U.S. banks. The National Giro has yet to make a significant impact on the market (only £49 million in June 1970). Since 1959 there has been a huge increase in foreign currency deposits from less than £1,000 million to more than £40,000 million (see pp. 95–107 on Euro-dollars), and the total number of banks, including foreign banks, has increased by more than half. All these developments have had considerable significance for the Bank of England in its application of monetary controls. Of the banks dealing in foreign currencies the *Quarterly Bulletin* stated 'their ability to switch in and out of foreign currency has had implications for the balance of payments, interest rate policy

and exchange control.' This has been recognized in the definition of 'eligible liabilities', which includes sterling obtained by switching from foreign currencies, against which the reserve assets ratio must now be calculated.

Control of other financial institutions

Even in 1959 the Radcliffe Report emphasized the point that as financial institutions other than the deposit banks came to provide more and more credit so the traditional means of control aimed largely at the deposit banks would be less and less effective in restricting the total supply of money and would be unfair to the deposit banks with whom these other institutions were in competition. The banks are requested to act against their own commercial interests when the others are not. For the Bank of England there is no easy solution to the problem for the means of control used with the deposit banks cannot easily be applied to these other institutions. We have seen that traditional controls operate through the deposit banks' balance sheets, i.e. cash ratio and liquidity reserve assets ratio. The other institutions have not until recently had to maintain similar ratios or balance sheets. The Radcliffe Report advocated policies designed to influence the cost or availability of credit flows to the various sectors as a means of overall control. These controls have to be specific and direct with exemptions defined in detail. But frequent *use of H.P. controls* has been criticized as arbitrary and damaging for its heavy impact on specific industries. When circumstances demanded more severe restraint than could be achieved by acting on cash and liquidity ratio direct controls and the *imposition of lending ceilings* were introduced. But ceilings on lending related to each bank's position on some arbitrary date and this, it was claimed, stifled competition. This argument seemed to be accepted for in the new arrangements for competition and credit control quantitative restrictions of this sort have been dropped. In the past the Bank of England has issued its *directives* to the clearing banks alone, but now they are addressed to all groups of banks and to a wide range of financial institutions. Under the new arrangements the Bank will continue to make qualitative requests to these institutions, many of which are now also required to maintain cash deposits at the Bank. They also make regular returns to the Bank giving information on their activities. The Bank does not have legal powers to enforce these directives but its position as the recognized representative of the City and the various services it provides as well as the weapon of special deposits give a considerable amount of influence over all these institutions. All the following bodies wrote to the Select Committee commenting favourably on existing arrangements whereby government monetary policy is carried out through the Bank of England rather than directly by the Treasury: the Bankers Association and the Committee of the London Clearing Bankers; the London Discount Market Association; the Accepting Houses Committee; the Issuing Houses Association; the Stock Exchange Council; the Committee of Scottish Bank Managers; the British Insurance Association; the Building Societies Association; the Association of Investment Trust Companies; and the Finance Houses Association. The Bank also issues directives to the I.C.F.C. and the Finance Corporation for Industry. But not all authorities consider the arrangements satisfactory. In a memorandum to the Select Committee Lord Balogh wrote that the Bank of England's 'intense publicity in favour of a larger share for monetary policy in the government's economic strategy has been strongly biased and objectionable'. He argued that the Bank provided a much more powerful representation of City interests in the government than vice-versa. Clearly these roles are not always easy to reconcile. The new arrangements are discussed in more detail in Chapters 7 and 8.

Cash deposits scheme

Before the new arrangements brought within the direct control of the monetary authorities the banks and financial institutions other than clearing banks a scheme was floated which went halfway towards this position. This *cash deposits* scheme was similar to Special Deposits giving the Bank a weapon with which to affect the earnings of these institutions as well as their liquidity. The scheme has been superseded by the new controls.

The Bank reserves the right to be selective among the institutions in issuing its directives. In his speech to the Building Societies Association in May 1969 the Governor of the Bank said 'virtually all their lending is within the priority categories and I have been able to spare them completely from the ceilings on their business which I have had to apply to the banks and finance houses'. But he took the opportunity to warn them not to extend their lending activities to the consumer goods sector or to take on banking functions. Moreover anyone about to applaud the generosity of the Bank to the building societies should remember that house building is particularly sensitive to changes in interest rates.

The new markets for money

There are other factors which complicate the task of the Bank in carrying out monetary policy, e.g. the development of the new financial markets and particularly the switching into and out of foreign currencies mentioned earlier. There are now more than 120 overseas banks with offices in London and all the major deposit banks have subsidiaries or associates which give them access to funds from these markets. (See Chapter 6, on inter-bank loans, local authority loans, Euro-currencies, certificates of deposits.) Professor Bain believes such credit expansion based on short term deposits from abroad to be particularly pernicious, as these funds are often withdrawn in a foreign exchange crisis. Lord Balogh criticizes the Bank of England for failing to give a more positive lead to participants in the market for Euro-currencies, and for failing to control the direction of its development. He points out that British financiers are involved in the market to the probable tune of $20 billion. If domestic borrowers have access to these funds through various financial intermediaries the task of the Bank in limiting credit expansion is clearly not made easier. Professor Bain suggests that while all foreign and domestic financial institutions should be able to compete freely for funds and lending business they should be subject to aggregate controls, and regulation should be related to classes of *assets* and *liabilities*. He would like the Bank to have powers to control *any* inflow or outflow of funds from overseas, and powers to prevent sharp changes in the division of the supply of capital funds between the broad sectors of the economy during limited periods of time.

Interest rate policy

One final complication for the Bank is the need to reconcile the conflicting aims of interest rate policy. The Radcliffe Report considered debt management to be the fundamental task of the central bank. The problem is that circumstances which call for restrictions on lending to control the level of economic activity have often coincided with a growing need for government borrowing. (See Professor Newlyn's comment below – on p. 25.) A rise in interest rates designed to discourage credit expansion inevitably increases the cost of government borrowing. While Radcliffe believed that monetary policy operating through interest rates was not only the 'proper method of affecting financial conditions and eventually, through them, the level of demand', but also 'an instrument of singular potency', other authorities have questioned this view. The Bank itself states that 'the movement of interest rates required to achieve adequate liquidity absorption through debt operations may be so large that a rapid or seemingly arbitrary adjustment could permanently damage the willingness of investors to hold gilts, compounding the difficulties of monetary management in the future'. (*B.E.Q.B.* December 1969). Although potential borrowers are in the short run rather insensitive to all but large changes in interest rates it is clear that even moderate changes in interest rates have a substantial effect on the direction and level of flows of capital funds, but here the role of expectations must be emphasized. It is what investors expect to happen to interest rates that is important, for this can cancel out the actions of the Bank or greatly accentuate them. It is also important that the overall desire to hold gilts is not fundamentally affected, particularly with the Euro-currency and other markets competing for funds. A reduction in the proportion of government debt in the total assets of the banks, as has occurred in recent years, reduces the effectiveness of Bank of England controls, which operate by influencing the deposit banks' lending rather than by reducing the cash base of the system. But the greater willingness to allow interest rates to reach higher levels as the result of market and other pressures, which has also been a feature of recent years, has given the Bank greater flexibility in tactics for debt management. Three recent developments have increased this flexibility. In the first place the Bank now sells 'tap stocks' to the best bids from the market instead of to any buyers who are prepared to pay the stated price. This system reduces rigidity of prices and interest rates. Secondly, instead of the official buying price for government bonds within three months of maturity being tied to the Treasury bill rate the Government Broker can now receive offers for the bonds. Thirdly, the discount houses syndicated bid for Treasury Bills has been abolished.

It is argued that the Bank's interest rate policy should not be worked out with the narrow object of influencing the banks' lending as the prime objective. Changes in interest rates must be considered with the flows of capital funds in the economy as a whole in mind. In fact this is the stated recent practice of the Bank (see *B.E.Q.B.* December 1969). 'The authorities stance has generally been to decide on an interest rate policy broadly appropriate to the general aims of economic policy at the time rather than using it to enforce a particular level of cash reserves irrespective of the wider effects of such a policy'. Undoubtedly, a highly important underlying concern of the Bank in its policy is to preserve a good and orderly market for government debt. The new arrangements for control of credit have done nothing to indicate a change in the view of authority of the importance of interest rates in monetary policy.

Is monetary policy effective?

The Radcliffe Committee concluded in 1959 that monetary measures by themselves would not take effect quickly enough unless used with such force that the side-effects would be critical. The measures must therefore be used as part of a general policy which includes fiscal measures and physical controls for without cooperation one might work against the others. The controls cannot be used to produce fine changes of balance. Much more information and understanding will be needed before a real measure of certainty attends their use. Within the general economic policy the monetary aspects played a permissive role in the immediate post-Radcliffe period. Occasionally (during the 'stop' part of the 'Stop-Go' cycle) permissiveness gave way to short periods of stringent controls. The story of the use of high interest rates and other severe measures over a prolonged period belongs to the second half of the decade since Radcliffe. The change of emphasis shown by the increasing part played by monetary measures in the general economic policy to limit the growth of demand is commented upon by the Bank in its *Quarterly Bulletin*: 'as the limits of effectiveness of fiscal policies, incomes policies and exchange controls appeared to be more nearly reached, the relative emphasis placed on monetary policy increased'.

Professor Newlyn and others have exposed the contradiction of a policy based on the control of the money supply when the 'open back door' lending tradition of the Bank of England allowed the institutions of the money market to meet their debt obligations even when other weapons are being used to restrict their funds. The authorities took steps in 1972 to exercise greater control on this last resort lending. Control of the money supply can only be effectively achieved if the public sector is in surplus. So the use of the traditional weapons of the Bank have in the past been rendered ineffective by deficits in public sector financing, which necessitated increased government borrowing, with the attendant increase in expansion of credit. Professor Newlyn argues that monetary policy will play a much more valuable part in overall economic policy at a time when a public sector surplus makes control of credit a possibility. In the financial year 1969–70 the public sector was in surplus to the extent of some £550 million, a position that had not been achieved since the war, and following a deficit of £450 million in 1968–69. That the Bank of England recognized the importance of this swing is clear from the Report for 1969–70: 'The movement from deficit into surplus by the public sector was one very important reason for the stringent monetary conditions during the financial year, and for the contraction of domestic credit . . .' It has been no easier to assess the effectiveness of monetary policy in the period 1970–73. The public sector moved strongly back into deficit; measures designed to give greater freedom to the banking sector coincided with other pressures to produce a dramatic rise in the money supply, and the government responded by the introduction of physical controls.

The Callaghan Government set clear guidelines for control of the growth of the money supply. Between the end of 1975 and the end of 1978 M_1 had expanded from £16 billion to £25 billion, while M_3 had risen from £36 billion to £49 billion. The Chancellor Denis Healey had the unenviable task of allowing the money supply to expand fast enough not to exacerbate the unemployment problem, but not so fast as to fuel inflation. The Bank of England was able to report that growth of sterling M_3 had been kept 'slightly below the 8–12 per cent target range'.

2.
THE COMMERCIAL BANKS

A new spirit is alive in the world of the commercial banks which is likely to produce a profound change in their market behaviour in the next few years. It would be foolish to pretend that the market form in commercial banking is anything other than a powerful oligopoly, but developments in the last decade have begun to erode this position, and a new spirit of competition is alive. This spirit has been injected from outside and nurtured within. The growth of competition from institutions which, while not commercial banks, were certainly interested in much of their business and were anxious to attract deposits from the commercial banks' customers brought about a gradual awareness that a fundamental rethinking of their position was necessary. It is this rethinking of the policies and practices which is needed to meet the challenge of the foreign banks, the merchant banks, the finance houses, and the other competitors in the market for money which has in turn made the commercial banks more aware of the competition among themselves. The authorities have given a boost to this renaissance of competition in the banking by helping to create freer conditions through the arrangements for competition and credit control of 1971. We will see in more detail later what have been the effects of this new spirit on the activities of the banks and the structure of the industry. In a recent book, *Men and Money*, Paul Ferris has shown how this new spirit is gradually infiltrating even the most conservative corners of commercial banks, both joint stock and private, throughout Europe, and how the British banks are in many cases leading the way, even if, as later chapters show, it was the United States banks' entry into Europe which speeded up the process. The invasion of London and other European financial capitals by American and Japanese banks has been primarily to take part in the Euro-dollar market, but once established these subsidiaries turn their attention to any business which will bring a good profit on activities. The market for money has become, much more than ten years ago, an international market. The commercial banks can no longer feel happily secure in their domestic market (see Table 1 below), nor can they presume that

Table 1. CURRENT AND DEPOSIT ACCOUNTS IN U.K. BANKING SECTOR (£M.)

Year	*Total*	*Total U.K. Residents*	*Total Deposit Banks*	*Government*	*Local Authorities*	*Public Corporations*	*Financial Institutions*	*Companies*	*Discount market*	*Accepting Houses Overseas and other Banks*
1966	15753	11197	10230	157	186	64	536	2802	119	5404
1967*	18493	12549	11128	164	186	73	699	3223	130	7235
1968	22221	13515	11741	187	134	69	750	3518	121	10349
1969	27493	13959	11789	196	159	102	942	3320	109	15559
1970	32250	15261	12768	228	160	113	1162	3536	204	19220
1971	37885	16943	14552	222	200	122	1271	4113	399	22859
1972†	50936	21472	18143	261	200	164	2243	5694	386	32307
1973†	71490	28179	23081	337	181	207	3112	8025	194	48092
1978	159458	48026	?	676	331	396	7356	14777	88	?

* After devaluation.
† Certain new contributors included in the series.

Source: *Bank of England Statistical Abstract.*

Table 2. THE BIG FOUR

	BARCLAYS		LLOYDS		NATIONAL WESTMINSTER		MIDLAND
1968	Martins	Barclays	Wm. Deacons (1930) Glyn Mills (1939)	Lloyds National (1966)	Nat. Provincial District (1962) Coutts (1920)	Westminster	Midland
	British Mutual (1951) Lands & Yorks (1928) Equitable (1927) E. Reed & Sons (1925) Cattle Trade (1923) Halifax Commercial (1920) Cocks, Buddulph (1919) Palatine (1919) Bank of Liverpool (1918)	Gunner (1953) Union Bank of Manchester (1940) Gillett (1922) Cox (France) (1922) British Linen (1919) London Provincial (1918) South Western (1918)	British Overseas (1944) Anglo International (1944) Child (1924) Holt (1923)	Royal Bank of Scotland (1966) National Commercial Bank of Scotland (1966) Lewis's (1967) (from Martins) National Bank of New Zealand (1966) Cox (1923) Henry S. King (1923) Fox Bros., Fowler (1921) West Yorkshire (1919) Capital & Counties (1918)	Isle of Man (1961) Guernsey (1923) Dingley (Launceston) and Perse (Okehampton) (1922) Coutts (1920) Northamptonshire Union Bank (1919) Richards (Llangollen) (1919) Sheffield Banking (1918)	Guernsey Commercial Stilwell & Sons (1923) Beckett (Leeds & York) (1921) Nottingham & Nottinghamshire (1919) Parr's Bank (1918)	Northern (1965) N. of Scotland (1924) Clydesdale (1920) London & Joint Stock (1918)

Dates in brackets indicate when the bank joined the group.
Compiled from *Monopolies Commission Reports*

certain kinds of business belong to them exclusively. The various money markets are coming closer together. The flow of funds into Euro-dollars, to local government, to the Inter-bank market, to the government bond market, or into bank deposits is the concern of a large number and a wide range of different financial institutions and not least the commercial banks. It has not been a significant feature of the past activities of the commercial banks to compete in these markets and while their experience of competing overseas through their subsidiaries is not inconsiderable a new body of expertise is rapidly being built up. The banks are surprising many observers (and perhaps themselves) by their adaptability to new forms of business. The next decade will no doubt see a further reorientation of the business of the commercial banks with their international business increasing in significance compared with their domestic business. At the same time customers who have traditionally thought only of the commercial banks as a resting place for their deposits, and as an agent for their payments, and a source for loans, will increasingly be turning to the alternatives offered by the Post Office Giro and the other institutions already mentioned. We will examine the ways in which the banks are meeting international and domestic competition later in the chapter.

First we must outline the basic functions of the commercial banks in the present day and their part in the money markets. In Britain the commercial banks, which are deposit banks, are called clearing banks, because they are members of the London Clearing House, which handles all their cheque transfers. Until recently there were eleven clearing banks with more than 13,000 branches. Table 2 on page 26 shows how these eleven banks have merged into what is popularly known as 'the Big Four'. Table 3 shows some of the connections between the Big Four and banks in Scotland and Northern Ireland.

Table 3. ASSOCIATED BANKS

London Clearing Bank	*Scotland*	*N. Ireland*
Barclays	British Linen	
Lloyds	National Commercial Bank of Scotland	
	Royal Bank of Scotland	
National Westminster	Bank of Scotland	Ulster
Midland	Clydesdale	Belfast
		Northern

The clearing banks' first essential function is to attract customers' deposits for which they pay a rate of interest, until 1971 2 per cent below Bank rate, on deposit accounts but pay no interest on sums held in current accounts. It is necessary to give seven days notice for withdrawals from deposit accounts, but customers can withdraw on demand from their current accounts, or transfer sums from this account by use of a cheque. The size of the deposits they attract is a fundamental indicator of the success of a clearing bank. Without these deposits the banks are unable to make loans, the second essential function of a clearing bank. The object of the banks is, of course, to make profits so while they pay depositors a rate less than the base lending rate they usually charge their borrowers a rate above that. The rate charged to borrowers varies according to the nature of the loan and the standing of the customer, only the most favoured customers being charged 'base rate'. The banks have to allocate part of their funds for lending very carefully according to established banking conventions. The first 1½ per cent of their assets cannot be lent out but must be kept in the form of cash in their accounts at the Bank of England. Until 1971 this cash ratio, which then included all the banks' till money, had to be maintained above 8 per cent, as the table below shows.

Table 4. THE CASH BASE OF THE CLEARING BANKS 1964–1971 (£M.)

Year	*Total Cash*	*% of Deposits*	*At the Bank of England*
1964	696	8·1	249
1965	739	8·2	266
1966	767	8·2	263
1967	798	8·2	280
1968	851	8·2	309
1969	879	8·2	283
1970	826	8·1	185
1971 (July)	912	8·1	219

Source: Committee of London Clearing Bankers.

The next 11½ per cent or so has to be available to the banks at short notice in case of a need to adjust this cash position. At certain times in the year the banks' customers make heavier than normal demands for cash, perhaps to pay for Christmas presents, for summer holidays, to buy goods in the sales, or to settle outstanding tax bills.

At such times, particularly if, as in the last case, the cash is not finding its way quickly back into the clearing banks' holdings, the banks have to be able to call in loans quickly to restore their cash position. A significant proportion of the banks' assets are therefore held in the form of balances with other U.K. banks, loans to the discount houses, and other financial institutions, on a very short term basis. In practice the greater part of the item 'money at call and short notice' is not frequently recalled but is made available to the discount houses for periods varying from a few days up to three months. The longer the period the higher the rate of interest it carries.

A small part of this very short term money is inevitably very liquid. These are the balances which individual banks are left with at the end of the day's business of sorting cheques and making settlements at the London Clearing House. One day Barclays may find they have a surplus on the day's dealing of £1 million, and this they make available as *privilege money* to the discount houses on a day to day basis. If Barclays are not in deficit to other banks after the next day's dealings the discount house borrowers may be allowed to renew the loan for another day, but if they are in deficit the money will be drawn in to settle the debts with the other banks. Surplus funds will also be lent at short notice in the other money markets.

The rate of interest which the banks earn on 'bills discounted' is higher than that for other reserve assets. The banks hold various types of bills: U.K. Treasury bills, commercial bills and other bills, which includes local government bills as well as the Treasury bills of the Northern Ireland government. By convention the banks do not tender directly for Treasury bills but buy them from the discount houses seven days or more after their issue. A discussion of the apparently unjustifiable and certainly unique system whereby the discount houses borrow money from the banks to buy bills which they then sell back to the banks occurs in a later chapter. The life of the Treasury bill before it matures is usually for ninety-two days but there are other bills for two months, four months or six months, and the life span of commercial bills is even more variable, according to the nature of the business which it is financing. Again the rule, the longer the period the higher the rate of interest, applies, and in the market for bills there is another rule, the greater the risk (of the bill not being honoured) the higher the rate of interest. Thus on January 15 1971 when Bank rate was 7 per cent buying rates in the discount market were:

Table 5. DISCOUNT RATES

Treasury Bills		*Bank Bills*			*Fine Trade Bills*			
2 mths	3 mths	2/3 mths	4 mths	6 mths	3 mths	4 mths	6 mths	
$6\frac{3}{4}$	$6\frac{25}{32}$	$8-8\frac{1}{8}$	$8\frac{1}{16}-\frac{1}{4}$	$8\frac{1}{8}-\frac{3}{8}$	$8\frac{1}{2}-9$	$8\frac{1}{2}-9$	$8\frac{3}{4}-9\frac{1}{2}$	%

Bank bills are those bills accepted by houses of the highest standing. Fine Trade bills are those bills accepted simply by a trader.

The banks' holdings of the different types of bills have varied a good deal since the war, and while this will be discussed in more detail later, it should be said here that the main trends have been (*a*) a revival in the importance of the commercial bill and a decline in the massive dominance of the Treasury bill, particularly from 1960–65, (*b*) a considerable growth in holdings of other bills (particularly local government bills) and the continued decline of the Treasury bill since 1965. These are illustrated in Table 6. There has been a reduction in the proportion of assets held in all sterling bills

Table 6. BILLS DISCOUNTED BY LONDON CLEARING BANKS 1964–1971

	Total	*Treasury Bills*	*Commercial Bills*	*Other Bills*
1964	1155	790	283	82
1965	1115	653	368	93
1966	1134	689	343	103
1967	1056	564	357	135
1968	995	468	341	186
1969	862	294	274	294
1970	921	206	311	404
1971 (July)	1228	202	489	537

Averages of monthly figures in £m.

Source: *Financial Statistics H.M.S.O.*

discounted since the liquidity ratio of 28 per cent was replaced by a reserve assets ratio of $12\frac{1}{2}$ per cent particularly as no more than 2 per cent of liabilities can be held in commercial bills for reserve purposes. The item 'bills discounted' has traditionally been included in the liquidity ratio because given the existence of a ready market for discounted bills the banks can easily dispose of these bills to raise cash to meet its debts if there is need to do so, though it may not be to the banks' advantage to sell bills they hold as they will be missing the chance of further profit on the bills. In March 1973 there were but £610 million of bills discounted.

The banks are now required to maintain a reserve assets ratio of 12½ per cent where at one time they had observed a 28 per cent liquidity ratio. But just as the average monthly figure for the liquidity ratio of all the London clearing banks taken together did not fall

Table 7. LIQUIDITY RATIOS

Year	1964	1965	1966	1967	1968	1969	1970*	1971 July
Liquidity Ratio	30·3	30·7	31·0	30·6	30·5	30·1	31·7	32·0

*In 1970 some changes were made by the banks in their accounting procedures because they had been required to disclose their profits for the first time. In effect, reducing gross deposits by £350 million, was to inflate the ratio of liquid assets to deposits.

Source: *Financial Statistics, H.M.S.O.*

below 30 per cent in any year between 1948 and 1971, so reserve assets have been maintained well above the required 12½ per cent.

Table 8. RESERVE ASSETS RATIO

£m.	*Eligible Liabilities*	*Reserve Assets*	*Ratio %*
December 1971	10946	1760	16·1
December 1972	13311	2135	16·0
March 1973	14569	2072	14·2
August 1973	16308	2117	13·0
November 1977	40223	6064	15·1
November 1978	44635	6033	13·5

Source: *B.E.Q.B.*

The banks hold surplus liquid assets partly because of their assessment of possible short-term cash requirements partly because of the flexibility which this gives them, and partly because it provides a buffer against those weapons of the monetary authorities, like special deposits, which are aimed at squeezing the banks reserve assets ratio. It safeguards them from having to call in profitable advances and investments to restore the ratio.

Table 9. CONSTITUTION OF TOTAL RESERVE ASSETS ON 15TH NOVEMBER 1978

Balances with Bank of England (other than Special Deposits)	413
U.K. and Northern Ireland Treasury bills	1041
Money at call	2873
British government stocks with less than one year to maturity	726
Local Authority bills	183
Commercial bills	798
	6034

Source: *B.E.Q.B.*

We have seen that the purpose of keeping a significant proportion of the banks' assets in fairly liquid form is so that the banks can easily meet any demand for cash made on them by their customers. Even though it would be impossible for the banks to meet the demand if all their customers wanted to withdraw their deposits at the same time, it is important that each individual customer believes that his bank will meet his demands for cash immediately on demand. Without this trust the banking system could not operate.

In reality the banks have long enjoyed a position of complete trust so that, as many writers have pointed out, the banks could easily meet all likely demands even with the reduced liquidity (reserve assets) ratio. The position has been complicated though by the use of monetary weapons by the Bank of England which operate through this ratio. In his book, *Competition in Banking*, Brian Griffiths argues that cash and liquidity requirements should be abolished. It is certainly unlikely that the clearing banks would, in the interests of greater competition, endanger this position in the public confidence by maintaining too low a level of liquid assets. L. C. Mather at the Cambridge Seminar for the Institute of Bankers put it like this: '. . . the prime function of the clearing bank as a lender in this country must always be to afford only short term accommodation when required for approved purposes. The extent to which we depart from this basic rule depends on government policy, liquidity needs and profitability.'

The reserve assets then are more significant as items to maintain the banks' reputation for secure handling of customers' deposits and to facilitate the authorities' control of the money supply, than as a means of raising profits. A further item is entirely an instrument of monetary control and that is special deposits. These were first introduced by the Bank of England in July 1958. The clearing banks (and the Scottish banks) were required under the scheme to deposit sums of money with the Bank of England amounting in the first instance to 1 per cent of gross deposits. These deposits are not at the free disposal of the banks and are therefore not part of the liquid assets. The Bank of England pays the banks interest on their deposits equal to the current Treasury bill rate. Since 1965 when special deposits were recalled at ½ per cent (after being previously released in November 1962) the rate has been stepped up until it reached 3½ per cent in November 1970. In the last quarter of 1971 special deposits were repaid, but late in 1972 calls of up to 3 per cent were made on banks and the other institutions now included in the scheme.

Table 10. SPECIAL DEPOSITS 1965–1971

April 1965	June 1965	July 1966	August 1966	May 1970	November 1970	September 1971	December 1972
½%	1%	1¼%	2%	2½%	3½%	repaid	3%

The Scottish Banks have, in the past, deposited at half the London rate, but this right was withdrawn in 1971 and the concession must now be applied for. In 1973 the Authorities introduced a differential rate between calls on domestic and calls on overseas deposits.

As an instrument to control the money supply special deposits have hardly been effective. The banks have rarely been in a position where the need to pay over to the Bank of England further special deposits has seriously affected its lending policy. No doubt the authorities could make special deposits a more effective weapon by tightly controlling the availability of the liquid assets but this would make it more difficult for the managers of the government debt because of a rise in interest rates. Special deposits were conceived as a means of supporting the authorities directives on the policies they expected the banks to carry out. When the banks failed to react quickly enough to a directive in 1970 the interest rate paid on special deposits was cut.

Traditionally it has not been the function of the clearing banks to undertake long term or risk lending, and while the new arrangements may well bring some change, in the past the banks have left this type of business in the hands of their subsidiaries and associates. The main earning assets of the banks are therefore their investments and their advances. The size of the banks' investments is largely determined by what is left over after they have met their liquidity ratio and the borrowing needs of their customers. If they wish to make more advances out of a given total of deposits they must realize some of their investments. If the proportion of reserve assets falls below 12½ per cent the position is likely to be corrected by realizing some of the investments. As a result of changes in 1971, the banks have been able to release funds from liquid assets and considerably expand their investment and advances.

At the end of 1958 the investments of the banks were divided in the main evenly between government bonds with up to five years to run to maturity (£985 million) and government bonds with more than five years to run to maturity or undated stocks (£1,009 million). The amount of other investments was only £108 million. By September 1970 the proportion of investments in other securities particularly loans to local authorities had increased, while the total of investments had declined, and the proportion of the banks' assets held in the form of investments was a good deal down on 1958 (10·4 per cent c.f. 29·2 per cent).

Table 11. LONDON CLEARING BANKS' INVESTMENTS (£M.)

	Government Bonds		*Other Securities*	*Total*
	Up to 5 yrs	More than 5 yrs		
1958	985	1009	108	2493
April 1973	1011	177	244	1432
	Up to 1 yr	More than 1 yr		
1978	222	1734	1285	3019

The banks arrange their portfolio of investments so that at any given time some of the stocks are coming up to maturity. When these bonds have less than three months to run they can be regarded as liquid assets. The buying and selling and maturing of bonds is going on all the time so that there is a ready market dealing in massive sums. The banks use this market as a means of meeting the increased demand of customers for advances (the banks sell bonds), or of investing sums not taken up by their customers (the banks buy bonds). It may not always be profitable for the banks to sell bonds before maturity because a rise in interest rates (perhaps initiated by the authorities) would bring about a fall in price of bonds. This mechanism can be used by the authorities to prevent the banks from increasing advances by selling bonds, although higher interest rates would increase the cost of debt management.

In recent years there has been a considerable expansion in the banks' dealings in Negotiable sterling certificates of deposit. Over £5,300 million were outstanding in the banking sector in March 1973. These CDs are 'documents issued by a U.K. office of a British or foreign bank, certifying that a sterling deposit has been made with that bank which is repayable upon the surrender of the certificate at maturity. It also states the rate of interest and the date of repayment, and is negotiable by simple delivery.'[1] They were first issued in October 1968. Banks who issue them have in this way been able to raise large sums at a fixed rate of interest for a fixed period. The funds which are attracted from a wider range of sources cannot be withdrawn prematurely. To the holder they give an attractive rate of interest and they can be sold in the secondary market at the ruling market rates if there is an unexpected need for liquidity. The clearing banks holding CDs are therefore able to meet the two main objectives of liquidity and profitability; and while they do not qualify as reserve assets they may be subtracted from a bank's total deposit liabilities in the calculation of eligible liabilities. The table below shows the growth of the banks' holdings.

CLEARING BANKS' HOLDINGS OF CERTIFICATES OF DEPOSIT

	£CDS	(£m.)
October 1971	77	
October 1972	608	
April 1973	433	
October 1978	1370	

While the banks' function of lending to the government is largely fulfilled by its investments and liquid items, the functions of lending to industry, trade and the other sectors of the economy, and to other members of the community is catered for mainly by the banks' advances. This item has grown in importance relative to the other assets in the last decade: in 1958 it accounted for 29·5 per cent of gross deposits, in 1964 for 52·8 per cent and in September 1970 for

[1] *B.E.Q.B.*, December 1972

55·4 per cent. The total sums advanced by the clearing banks were £2,126 million in 1958, £4,325 million in 1964, £5,896 million in August 1970 and £11,302 million in April 1973. As the asset earning the highest rates of interest it is clearly a trend welcomed by the banks that the ratio of advances to gross deposits has been increased. But the banks must have one eye to the overall liquidity and security of their assets and the other to the desire of the authorities to prevent such an increase of advances by the banks that the inflationary pressures evident in the economy are boosted further. The tension which has grown up between the obvious self-interest of the banks (and their customers) to expand advances and the government's objective of controlling the expansion of the money supply has been a feature of recent banking history.

Bank Advances

There have been some notable changes in the distribution of the banks' advances as well as a growth in their importance relative to the other assets. The changes in distribution reflect, to a certain extent, changes which are evident in the whole economy:

(*a*) The growth of some industries (electrical, engineering) and certain sectors, while others are stagnant or even decline.

(*b*) The need for major reorganization in certain industries, often with government support, e.g. shipbuilding and steel.

(*c*) The effects of government economic policy and direction e.g. the greater support for export industries such as vehicles, and for firms setting up in development areas. Also government encouragement for a transfer of resources from services industries to manufacturing and government determination to control consumer expenditure.

(*d*) The increase in competition from other banks is a factor in the recent decline in the clearing banks' advances to the financial sector. (The figures given for this sector exclude funds placed through the specialized financial markets).

The *Quarterly Bulletin* gives an analysis of advances by the London clearing banks to U.K. residents for August 1970 and August 1978:

Table 12. BANK ADVANCES 1970 AND 1978

	Clearing Banks 1970 Aug. £m.	Clearing Banks 1978 Aug. £m.	All Banks 1970	% of total advances
Manufacturing				
Food, Drink, Tobacco	251·8	703	387·3	2·9
Chemicals	134·0	509	288	2·2
Metals	166·5	264	205·2	1·5
Electrical	326·6	397	436	3·3
Other engineering & metal	587·6	1023	800·7	6·0
Shipbuilding	201·2	404	254·1	1·9
Vehicles	343·7	257	440·1	3·3
Textiles, Leather, Clothing	267·0	485	350·7	2·6
Other manufacturing	330·2	807	503	3·8
Total Manufacturing	2608·6	4852	3665	27·7
Other Production				
Agriculture, forestry, fishing	445·0	1318	538·2	4·1
Mining, Quarrying	45·8	136	115·7	0·9
Construction	355·8	995	452·7	3·4
Total other Production	846·6	2449	1106·6	8·3
Financial				
H.P. Finance Companies	53·4	146	101·8	0·8
Property Companies	188·0	812	334·4	2·5
U.K. Banks	23·5	1001	64	0·5
Other financial	122·6	1122	501	3·8
Total Financial	387·5	2081	1001·2	7·6
Services				
Transport & Communications	111·0	389	216·0	1·6
Public Utilities & National Government	92·5	614	132·9	1·0
Local Government services	22·4	65	58·4	0·4
Retail Distribution	296·6	1041	357·7	2·7
Other Distribution	277·4	991	500·7	3·8
Professional, scientific & other services	430·4	1937	613·0	4·6
Total Services	1230·3	5037	1879·3	14·2

	Clearing Banks 1970 *Aug.* £m.	1978 *Aug.* £m.	*All Banks* 1970	*% of total advances*
Personal				
House Purchase	316·6	1187	400·2	3·0
Other Personal	462·6	2608	591·1	4·5
Total Personal	779·2	3796	991·3	7·5
Overseas Residents	44	—	4572·6	34·6
Total Advances	5896·2	18214	13215	100

Source: *B.E.Q.B.*

Services

The banks make advances to their customers either by opening a loan account or by allowing them to run up overdrafts. As a source of finance the banks are more important to private companies than to public companies who obtain only one-sixth of their funds from this source. It is a further function of the banks to provide services for its customers wherever it seems possible and desirable. The most important of these is to provide means of payment and transfer of money. They do this by:

(*a*) Allowing their customers to draw cheques. This is the means whereby far the greatest amount of payments are made. More than 700 million are cleared each year, with a total value of more than £700,000 million.

(*b*) Keeping stocks of coins and notes which customers can draw over the bank counter or through dispensing machines.

(*c*) Following the instructions given by their customers through standing orders to make regular payments.

(*d*) Issuing banking cards. Some of these enable the holder to pay for a purchase by a direct debiting of his bank account.

(*e*) Providing a giro system. Customers can use this system to settle a number of debts to different creditors using only one cheque.

Some of the other services performed by the banks include issuing travellers' cheques, and arranging the purchase of foreign currencies; the purchase or sale of securities through a broker; acting as executors of wills and trustees to settlements; providing a safe place for keeping valuables; assisting customers with income tax problems; giving customers advice about investments.

The term, the banks' profits, is often loosely used in a way which really means the banks' revenue. This revenue arises chiefly from the interest earned on the various kinds of loans which the banks make, from the discounts earned from holding bills, from the charges to customers for services rendered, and from the commissions earned for other business such as buying shares (through a broker) on the stock exchange. The banks' profits are in fact what remains out of revenue when all the banks' costs have been met. These costs include payments of interest to customers who deposit their funds with the bank, the cost of maintaining staffing and running some 12,600 branches of the London clearing banks, as well as the head office staffs and services, and the payment for services rendered to the banks by other financial institutions at home and overseas. Out of these profits a sum will probably go to the banks' reserves which are available to meet any contingency, and, in the case of the joint stock banks, the profits for distribution will then be paid to the shareholders. Since the requirement in the early 1970s that the banks, like every other public company, must disclose the true figures of profits and reserves, a good deal of the mystery surrounding these figures has evaporated.

Recent developments in commercial banking

'The banks are responding to the challenges presented by a rapidly changing financial scene', wrote Leonard Mather the chief general manager of the Midland Bank in the *Times Financial Review* for 1970. The pressures for change have come partly from the force of increased competition, partly from the emergence of new financial opportunities, and partly from the changing attitude of the authorities, who have been prepared to accept the changes.

The increase in competition to the clearing banks has come from the establishment by foreign banks of offices and subsidiaries in this country, and from the expansion of British financial institutions into new fields of business. The table below shows how the clearing banks' share of total deposits has declined in recent years (see also Table 1). A similar analysis of total advances would reveal a decline in the clearing banks' proportion of the total business. Out of total advances of just over £13,000 million in 1970, the clearing banks advanced nearly £6,000 million, but the other banks more than £6,700 million (Scottish banks account for the difference). This is the first time that other banks have exceeded the advances of the clearing banks. Compare this with the situation in August 1968 when the clearing banks advanced just over £5,100 million and the other banks £3,300 million.

Table 13. DEPOSITS OF CLEARING BANKS & OTHER BANKS

Year	*Clearing Banks*	*Accepting Houses*	*British Overseas*	*American Banks*
1965	9454	1030	1676	1432
1966	9501	1135	1811	2215
1967*	10262	1464	2300	3283
1968	10736	1877	2744	5301
1969	10724	2446	4183	9755
1970	10606	2990	5465	11416
1971	12194	3382	6672	13427
1972	16187	4289	9270	17515
1973	21632	5549	12766	25621
1974	25511	4819	14406	28733
1975	26551	5065		
1976	29486	6354		
1977	32694	6960		
1978	37104	8107		

* Devaluation

Source: *Financial Statistics, H.M.S.O., & Bank of England Statistical Abstract.*

In mid-1973 the clearing banks advanced about £11,000 million out of £26,000 million.

Although the clearing banks are well aware of the increased competition from foreign banks, which incidentally are free from many of the restraints imposed on the clearing banks, the main business of the foreign banks is in foreign currencies, and, although their business in sterling is increasing, they have not yet seriously challenged the main domestic business of the clearing banks. Their sterling interest is much more in the new financial markets for wholesale money, i.e. local authority lending and the interbank loan market. In 1967 the clearing banks still held 64 per cent of all sterling deposits while the acceptance houses held 5 per cent, the British overseas and Commonwealth banks 7 per cent, foreign banks and affiliates 2 per cent, other overseas banks 2 per cent and other banks 3 per cent. By 1971 all these institutions have increased their share of the market at the expense of the clearing banks, which now has about one-third. Just how far the situation has changed can be seen when this share is compared with that of 1918 (67 per cent), 1930 (73 per cent), 1936 (75 per cent), and 1951 (80 per cent). However this should be seen against the background of widely expanding business and the growth of new markets.

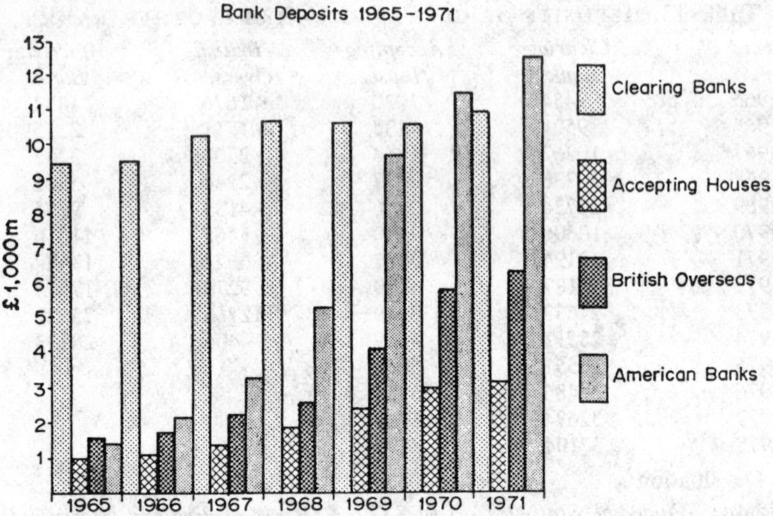

Until the arrangements of 1971 the banks met the challenge of increased competition and the development of new lines of business by establishing subsidiary companies and taking a share in other institutions to participate in the new business. These subsidiaries and associates were not subject to the same controls and restrictions as the parent banks. The banks have taken up interests in hire purchase, credit cards, Euro-currencies and Euro-bonds, investment management, unit trusts, and factoring. They claim to be able to meet virtually all the financial requirements of their customers through the wide range of services provided by their group of companies. By hiving off the specialist activities in this way the parent banks have been able to continue their own specialization in low risk, short to medium term, domestic lending, though they have been required by the authorities to provide finance at 5½ per cent fixed rate for certain export finance contracts insured by the Export Credits Guarantee Department. They have not welcomed these directives to provide this growing volume of funds at what is currently a low rate of interest and for longer terms than their usual business, particularly as it is not really profitable. The suggestion that the banks should participate in longer term lending of such a specialist nature as house purchase would be resisted by present day bankers. Leonard Mather makes this comment: 'With established liquidity conventions, and given the role they believe they are best fitted to play in the financial life of the country, the banks should continue their traditional practice of providing largely self-liquidating finance.' Some idea of the wide range of services provided by a banking group can be obtained from a perusal of this information taken from a Barclays advertisement headed:

'The Barclays Group is more than a group of banks. Barclays at home and overseas has the free world's largest branch banking network.

Barclays (London & International) Ltd: dealing in Euro-currencies and sterling deposits, and making medium term loans to industry for capital projects.

Barclays Export Finance Company Ltd: offering a specilized service to British exporters, especially non-recourse finance.

Barclays Bank Trust Co. Ltd: providing investment portfolio management, registrars and new issue, executor and trustee and personal taxation services.

Barclays Unicorn Ltd: managers of eight unit trusts.

Barclays Insurance Service Ltd: insurance broking service.

Baric Computing Services Ltd: a complete range of computer bureau applications.'

The Barclays Group includes in addition to the above:

Barclays Bank, Barclays bank D.C.O., Barclays bank S.A., Barclays bank of California, Barclays Overseas Development Corporation.

Associated Companies: Bank of Scotland, Banque de Bruxelles, United Dominions Trust, Banco del Desarrollo Economico Espanol, Societé Financière Européene, Intercontinental Banking Services Ltd.

The other big clearing banks offer similar services and have a similar range of subsidiary and associate companies. They have all supported the Industrial and Commercial Finance Corporation (I.C.F.C.) which specializes in medium term credit for industry, and the Finance Corporation for Industry which provides longer term finance. It is likely that the next decade will see an erosion of this division of business between the parent bank and its subsidiaries.

Foreign banks

The American banks are making a powerful impact on the banking scene in this country. Attracted to London in the first place by the lucrative Euro-dollar business they have gradually expanded in numbers and in their range of interests. Before 1960 there were fewer than ten branches of U.S. banks, now there are more than thirty branches and representative offices. While the big U.S. banks (the biggest in the world) open their own branches, some of the medium sized U.S. regional banks have set up co-operatively owned companies. In 1964 American banks branches in this country attracted less than £1,000 million of deposits of sterling and other currencies but by 1973 their gross deposits were over £20,000 million of which 3,000 was in sterling. The financial needs of the growing multinational, American dominated, corporations was another force which drove the American banks to participate in overseas banking, to acquire interests in foreign-owned merchant banking institutions to turn their attention increasingly to investment as well as to trade. In 1973 the American banks in Britain made more than £13,000 million of advances, mainly in currencies other than sterling.

The other foreign banks and their affiliates have not the enormous financial resources at home enjoyed by the American banks, but most of the major European and Japanese banks have begun to interest themselves in the Euro-currency business and this has brought them to London, the centre of the market. Before 1973 is out their gross deposits at branches in Britain will probably have reached £6,000 million, compared with approximately £500 million in 1965, and they will have advanced about £4,000 million. They keep quite considerable holdings in foreign currency with other U.K. banks often as trading balances. The funds attracted to this country by these banks help to swell Britain's reserves.

The establishment of foreign banks in London is greeted by British bankers as a welcome sign of the continued importance of the City as the centre of the financial world. These banks bring an increase of business which may be to the general advantage of City financial interests. Moreover British banks have reciprocated by expanding their banking business overseas, and countries with branches in Britain are less likely to deal unfavourably with British banks on their territory. Although these foreign banks are in competition with British banks in attracting deposits and making advances this competition is blunted in a number of ways. Sometimes the foreign banks are partners with British banks in financing projects at home or overseas. Sometimes they cooperate in setting up subsidiary firms, and sometimes foreign based companies with plant in this country rely for their finance partly on the bank of their own country with a branch in this country, and partly on the branch of a British bank which may be near their British based factory. It should be remembered that the British banking system is a branch while many other countries, like the U.S., have a largely unit based system. The com-

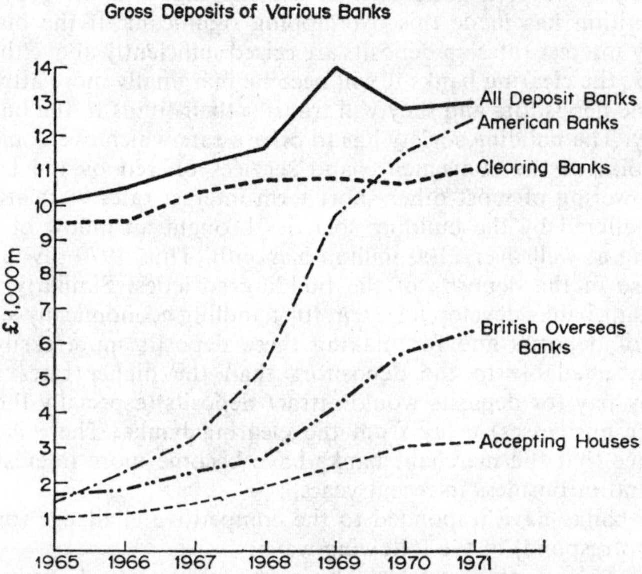

petition from foreign banks in Britain, both real and threatened, is a powerful force for change on the present day banking scene.

Other financial institutions

The competition from other financial institutions in this country both bank and non-bank is at the present time even more strongly felt than foreign competition particularly in domestic business. Each clearing bank has to consider very carefully the effect of its actions on the other clearing banks. They all have a similar share of the market, which displays most of the characteristics of an oligopoly. The clearing banks, merchant banks and other banks, and other financial intermediaries are all, directly or indirectly, in competition for deposits from the public and from business, even though they have their own specialist activities e.g. the building societies attract mainly longer term deposits, the merchant banks deal in larger units (wholesale money) and the clearing banks attract short term money which customers may need to obtain quickly to settle their debts.[1]

[1] There has been no remarkable expansion of H.P. advances during the 1960s but outstanding debt is running at over £1384 million. However the Big Four clearing banks have all bought themselves an interest

There is however a good deal of overlapping, and the growth of competition has made this overlapping significant. If the building society interest rates on deposits are raised sufficiently above the rate paid by the clearing banks it will become marginally more attractive to some depositors and they will transfer their funds to the building society. The building society has to offer a rate which overcomes the attraction of the convenience and services offered by the banks.[1] The lowering of most other short term interest rates in relation to those offered by the building societies brought an inflow of funds running at well over £100 million a month. Thus 1970 saw a huge increase in the deposits of the building societies. Similarly if the merchant banks develop a system for handling economically smaller units of deposits and for making these deposits more easily and quickly available to the depositors than the higher rates which already pay for deposits would attract deposits (especially those of smaller businesses) away from the clearing banks. There is some evidence that the merchant banks have become more interested in this kind of business in recent years.

The banks have responded to the competitive challenge (or they hope to respond) in the following ways:
(*a*) integration, (*b*) increased efficiency, (*c*) improved service, (*d*) diversification of business. (e) more competitive interest rates.
These lines of action are of course closely related.

Bank mergers

The second half of the 1960s saw a number of mergers which reduced the number of clearing banks trading independently from eleven to six. (See Table 2, p. 29.) The old pattern of the 'Big Five' and the 'Little Six' had remained undisturbed for thirty years. The mergers came in for close scrutiny from banking writers, and from the Prices and Incomes Board and the Monopolies Commission. It was the

[1] The building societies deposits are largely the 'shares' which depositors buy. These now amount to more than £8,000m. (c.f. 1960 less than £3,000m.) Mortgage advances are a similar figure.

in this business e.g. National Westminster own North Central Wagon. Just forty of the 1,500 or so finance houses make up the Finance Houses Association, and handle nearly 90 per cent of the total business. The Bank of England now issues directives to the F.H.A. and the houses must hold 10 per cent of their assets in liquid form. They can apply for bank status.

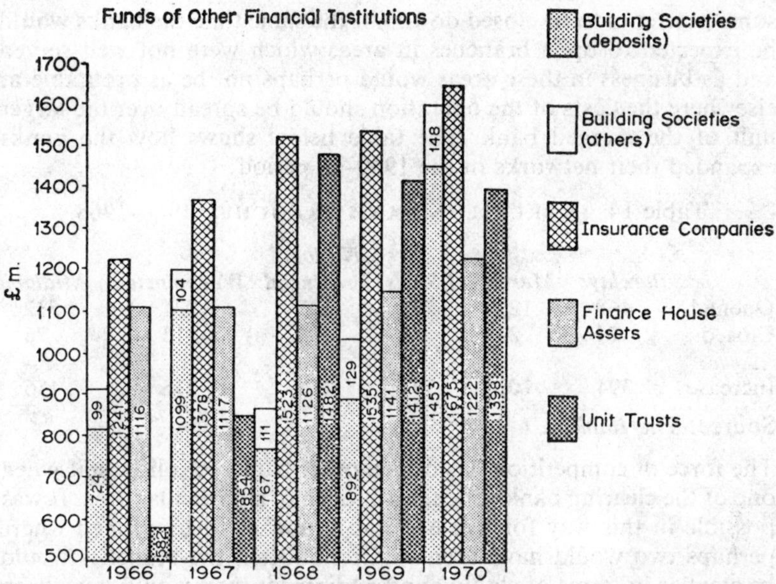

proposal to merge Barclays, Lloyds and Martins, which would have given the merged bank almost half of the market, which brought about the investigation by the Monopolies Commission. The arguments used by the three banks to support the merger will give the reader a clear picture of the possible advantages which arise from such integration.

Firstly, the time was propitious for reorganization in the banking world. All the major banks were beginning the process of computerization (though from this point of view the mergers might have taken place earlier). The currency of the country was about to change to a decimal unit.

Secondly, the mergers and take-overs had already produced a number of very large business units in industry and commerce e.g. British Leyland, I.C.I., and the process was likely to continue. The huge borrowing requirements and the other banking services required by these mammoth firms called for a parallel development of very large banking units.

Thirdly, some rationalization of the system of branch banking was long overdue. Banking authorities have argued for some time that some areas of the country were being overbanked, and that the best way to overcome the problem was by mergers which would enable some branches to be closed down. At the same time the banks would be expected to open branches in areas which were not well served and as business in these areas would perhaps not be as profitable as elsewhere the costs of the operation should be spread over the larger unit of the merged bank. The table below shows how the banks expanded their networks in the 1960–68 period:

Table 14. INCREASE IN BANK BRANCHES 1960–1968

	Barclays	*Martins*	*Lloyds*	*National Provincial*	*Westminster*	*Midland*
Opened	468	122	433	147	231	532
Closed	74	20	36	34	15	76
Increase	394	102	397	113	216	456

Source: *The Banker.*

The force of competition has driven other banks to follow suit when one of the clearing banks opened a branch in a particular area. It was possible in this way for five or more branches to be opened where perhaps two would have been sufficient. Often the branches would be smaller in terms of staffing and equipment than would have been the case if there had been fewer, and as a result unit costs were higher.

Fourthly, the mergers would enable each of the clearing banks to compete effectively in every part of the country without opening a batch of new branches. The table below sets out the share of the market held by the 'Big Four' in each of the regions. The bank may not be trading under the name given here, e.g. Lloyds interests in Scotland are represented by the National Commercial Bank and the Royal Bank, and in the North West by Williams Deacon's. (See Table 2).

Table 15. REGIONAL SHARE OF THE MARKET (%) 1970

	Scot.	N.E.	N.W.	Mids.	E.Ang.	London	S.E.	S.W.	Wales
Barclays	13	32	28	24	33	30	30	29	23
Lloyds	37	13	16	20	24	13	20	30	21
Nat. Westminster	*	18	36	31	21	35	28	31	24
Midland	21	27	19	25	22	17	19	20	32
Other	29	10	1			5	1		

*Nat. Westminster's interest in Scotland are represented by the Bank of Scotland.

Source: *The Banker.*

It seems reasonable to assume that mergers between the clearing banks will not only mean that fewer branches will have to be opened to meet competition from other banks, but also that some branches could be closed where other branches in the group could adequately cater for the banking needs of the area.

Fifthly, the increase in competition from non-bank institutions has provided an incentive to the clearing banks to link up for greater competitive strength. With the greater financial power that would result the merged banks would be able to meet the increased competition by improving their services and expanding into new lines of business.

Sixthly, the mergers would enable the British banks to meet the competition of the foreign banks. The huge resources of the American banks made such mergers particularly necessary. The prestige of the British banks in world markets would be restored by making them comparable in size with the American banks. They would be able to take the fight into these world markets and so gain for Britain valuable invisible earnings.

Seventhly, it would seem that the smaller the number of banks the easier would be the problem of control by the monetary authorities.

Finally, economies of scale would result from larger banks dealing with larger deposits from larger customers. There is little extra cost involved in servicing a large loan compared with a small one.

This point leads us to consider the fundamental argument that mergers lead to an increase in banking efficiency. Professor Kreps has stated that American experience suggests that 'further increases in size may be accompanied by further scale economies, but these are, for all practical purposes, insignificant.' It would certainly be unfortunate if economies of scale and economies of rationalization were only secured by a reduction in the range and standard of services, or accompanied by a considerable increase in charges to the small customer, but recent experience (Saturday closing) and higher current account changes suggests this may be happening.

Computers

The need to spread the considerable cost of installation and to make the optimum use of the computer has been an important factor favouring integration and the search for increased efficiency. In 1969 George Norman wrote in *Bankers Magazine*, 'The concentration of banks in Britain into large groupings will permit optimum use of the medium and by 1971 all branch banks are expected to be 'on-line' to central computers in a nation-wide hook up'. He went on to describe the reorientation of organization and practice within the banks which would result from this: the reduction in the number of clerks and greater union militancy, the increase in the number of skilled technicians, the decline in the status of the cashier, instant availability of information on customers from stored tape, the disappearance of the cheque, and so on. With wage bills, and until recently S.E.T. payments, among the highest in any line of business (see below) the reduction in staff made possible by computers could provide a valuable economy.

Table 16. WAGES AND S.E.T.* 1969

	Wages	*S.E.T.*
National Westminster	£67 million	£4·2 million
Barclays	£59 million	£4·0 million
Woolworths	£36 million	£4·0 million

* In 1973 with the introduction of V.A.T., S.E.T. was finally phased out.

There have been complaints that the use of computers depersonalize banking, and that the small customer will suffer, but the banks argue that a computerized system should enable them to improve such services as giro transfers, and to keep down charges to the customer. However when George Norman gazed into his crystal ball he saw the ancient craft of banking being replaced by computer decisions and some of the functions of money disappearing. He wrote '. . . the insertion of the money-card will automatically activate the computer to note the bank balance, and, if in debit, to make a lightning survey of the account including turnover, job and credit classification, securities held, total income, reports from credit agencies, other outstanding indebtedness and the history of previous borrowings. The decision whether or not to grant further credit is then made by the computer at the time of payment in accordance with programmed criteria including official monetary policy and the bank's liquidity position'.

In a market where price competition is virtually ruled out – the clearing banks operate almost identical interest rates and bank charges – the profitability of one bank compared to the others can only be increased by an increase in its efficiency which reduces its unit costs at a time when the unit costs of the other banks move less favourably. The introduction of computers is an attempt to increase efficiency and gain cost advantage at a time when operating costs were increasing rapidly (by more than 50 per cent in the 1960s) and when labour costs account for 70 per cent of the total. But this is not the only form taken by competition between the banks as the spate of advertising in the late 1960s showed. It resulted in a 25 per cent increase in the number of accounts and a 30 per cent increase in bank clearings, but also in such an escalation of advertising expenditure that the banks have recently begun to look for cut-backs in this quarter. Management consultants have been called in by some of the banks to advise on how their organization and management could be improved.

The report of the P.I.B.

The report of the Prices and Incomes Board in 1966 highlighted many of the developments mentioned above. The P.I.B. was, of course, chiefly concerned with bank charges, interest rates and the profits received by the banks. The Board pointed to four main determinants of the level of charges and rates. Firstly, the banks assessed the credit-worthiness of the customer. Secondly they attempted to cover the costs involved in the lending. Thirdly, there was an element of 'charging what the market can bear'. Fourthly, the banks recognized the right of certain borrowers to call on other services of the bank. But the Board found it anomalous that different rates were being charged to H.P. companies and insurance companies, and similarly that there were differences in the rates charged to nationalized industries and local authorities. Moreover they could see no reason for the collective agreements on advance rates. This cartel arrangement by the clearing banks came in for a great deal of criticism. This table of rates is taken from the P.I.B. report:

Table 17. RATES ON ADVANCES

Nationalized Industry (Treasury guarantee)	Bank Rate (min. 4%)
Local Authorities Building Societies Insurance Companies First Class Borrowers	Bank rate + ½% (min. 4½%) ('Blue Chip' rate)
Hire Purchase Companies	Bank rate + 1% (min. 6%)
Export loans (ECGD guarantee)	Bank rate (min. 4½%) up to 2 years Fixed rate 5½%, 2–15 yrs.
Other industrial, commercial and private borrowers	At discretion, but above Blue Chip rate
Personal loans	Usually Bank Rate + 2%

The P.I.B. objected to the veil of secrecy drawn around bank charges and bank profits: 'in the interests of more effective competition we think that the banks should desist from collective agreements and should publish individual tariffs of charges'. The banks have had the traditional right (not allowed to other public companies) of making hidden transfers to (or from) the reserves before publishing their profits. They argued that this helped to preserve public confidence both in the banks and in sterling. It enabled them to operate on the same footing as their foreign competitors, and to safeguard the interests of big customers whose fortunes were tied closely with the banks. The P.I.B. recommended disclosure of true profits and this was eventually accepted by the banks in 1970. This table which gives an index of true and hidden profits for the clearing banks from 1961 to 1965 was taken from the P.I.B. report, and has 1951 (= 100) as the base year.

Table 18. BANK PROFITS 1961–1965 (£M.)

Year	Actual Profit		Published Profit
	Before tax	*After tax*	
1961	299	367	273
1962	250	299	274
1963	252	310	283
1964	311	369	345
1965	417	587	550

Most of the P.I.B. recommendations were concerned with increasing competition – the abolition of common rates, greater competition for deposits, extension of lending activities, and so on, but they also commented on the level of bank reserves which they thought might be excessive, and on the increase in profits which resulted from a rise in Bank rate and no extra effort on the part of the banks. They also came out in support of 'further amalgamations among the banks [which], carried through to the appropriate point, could permit some rationalization of existing networks', and indicated that the Bank of England and the Treasury would not (as had been assumed) obstruct further amalgamation. With the introduction of the new arrangements for competition and credit control and subsequent developments in 1972 and 1973 most of the P.I.B. recommendations have been implemented.

The Monopolies Commission on the bank merger

In the event obstruction did not come from this quarter. We have already described how certain mergers went ahead, but the proposal for a merger between Lloyds, Barclays, and Martins was referred to the Monopolies Commission. The merger would have meant that National Westminster and Midland would have had about a quarter each of the market, while the merged bank would have had the other half. The Commission like the Board put the emphasis on competition. '. . . we consider that competition among banks is in the public interest and that such competition as there is among clearing banks is likely to be keener with large clearing banks of roughly comparable size than with three banks with one as large as the other two combined'. The majority of the Commission could see little more than marginal benefit to the public interest, and a risk from the reduction in the number of sources of finance, particularly as the fast growing small and medium sized businesses were the ones most likely to suffer. The minority report argued in favour of the merger largely on the grounds of the savings (through rationalization) which might be achieved, and they thought that competition was more likely in a situation of some inequality of size. The problem of holding down costs was seen by the Commission to be a major problem in the coming years, and they hoped that this might be staved off by the reduction in the number of branches by perhaps a 1000, giving a saving of some £10 million. The sharp rise in bank costs has indeed occurred.

A notable feature of the annual reports of the clearing banks in recent years has been the growing intensity of the complaints about the inhibiting effect of the actions of the monetary authorities. The clearing banks are certainly in the front line of government attack on inflationary pressures, and it has long been argued that the weight of monetary measures falls unfairly on the banks. Some efforts have now been made to bring non-bank financial institutions within the ambit of the directives. The Radcliffe Report recognized that the financial institutions are competing in a single market for credit, and recommended that serious attention be paid to controls over lending by financial institutions other than banks: they wanted a combination of measures which can strike promptly and vigorously at the central points of the financial system. The P.I.B. report recommended that all deposit taking institutions should be subject to appropriate requirements with regard to their capital reserves, to total obligations, and the ratio of liquid assets to deposit obligations.

A glance at the diary of some credit controls since 1964 will give some idea of the restrictions encountered by the banks.

Table 19. DIARY OF CREDIT CONTROLS

1964 December: Directives from the Bank of England to restrict loans, particularly those for hire purchase, property development and personal use.

1965 April: Special deposits 1 per cent called, liquid assets thus reduced by £100.

1965 May: Directive that advances should not expand more than 5 per cent 1965–66.

1966 February: Directive to freeze advances at 105 per cent March '65.

July: Special deposits doubled.

August: Directive that banks must if necessary withdraw from present commitments to maintain 105 per cent ceiling.

1967 April: 105 per cent ceiling lifted.

November: Bank advances limited to all but priority (exporters, development areas, etc.) borrowers.

1968 May: Directive to limit all private sector loans to 4 per cent above November 1967 level.

1969 January: Directive to limit all but priority lending to 98 per cent November 1967.

June: Banks penalised for failing to meet directive, rate on Special Deposits cut by half.

1970 April: Some easing allowed to 105 per cent November 1967 level.

July: Sharp reminder that banks are expected to keep within this.

1971: Ending of ceilings in favour of other forms of control.

1972 December: 2 calls for Special Deposits amounting to 3 per cent of total deposits.

1973 November: minimum lending rate raised to 13 per cent and a further 2 per cent of total deposits required for Special Deposits.

The bankers believed that their growth rates were restricted by these measures at a time when other financial institutions have expanded rapidly. They regarded the arbitrary ceilings imposed by the directives as 'a deplorable clog on enterprise and competition' affecting services and profits. The banks could hardly have been expected to welcome a system of monetary control which asked them to act in the interests of the country but against their own commercial interests, when the same did not apply to all their competitors. They resented their position as the whipping boy of government economic policy.

Finally, how are the recent developments in commercial banking likely to affect the relationship between the banks and the discount market? The discount houses have traditionally used the funds which the clearing banks want to keep liquid, and the cash which is surplus after the days clearing as the major source of their finance. There are four main reasons why this position may be in the process of changing. Firstly, other banks and institutions are taking an interest in this market. Secondly, there is a growth of new markets competing for call money. Thirdly, there have been a number of bank mergers. Fourthly, much bank business has been put on to computers.

The merging of the clearing banks could affect the day-to-day surpluses, for where there are eleven banks there will be more surpluses than where there are six. The surpluses are now used within the groups and there will be a dovetailing of surpluses. The larger banks will be able to work closer to liquidity margins leaving less call money to be distributed. The introduction of computers will eventually speed up the process of bank clearing. Once same day clearing becomes established there could be no day-to-day surpluses to lend out. And how long will it be before the banks begin to compete directly in market for very short money? The new measures have done a good deal to produce an atmosphere in which competition in the banking sector is developing. Not only have the cartel arrangements between the clearing banks been ended but they have begun to expand their business in areas like consortium banking where they previously had not been directly involved. Chapter 8 traces some of these developments.

3.
THE DISCOUNT MARKET

The discount market consists of those institutions which are involved in buying, selling and holding Treasury bills and commercial bills. There is no physical market, but the diagram at the end of the chapter attempts to give a simplified picture of the relationship between the institutions and customers involved in the market. As with most of the other markets for money and near-money the Bank of England is as the sun at the centre of a galaxy of satellites. It manipulates and controls the market when public policy and national interests deems it necessary. The discount houses are the principal participants, and until recently the discounting of bills had been almost their sole activity. The accepting houses have many roles for they are merchant banks whose part in the market is to lend their name in order to guarantee commercial bills and their money to those who wish to discount bills. The Treasury is important as the determinant of the supply of Treasury bills, which are then issued by the Bank of England. The very short-term money which is the essential working capital of the market comes in the main from the commercial banks, although other institutions like the merchant banks, foreign and other banks are a regular source of funds. The commercial banks have another interest in the market as substantial holders of second hand bills. They also discount bills for their own customers. The foreign banks have begun to challenge the monopoly of the discount houses 'syndicate' which bids to take up the issue of Treasury bills each Friday.[1] A further development has been the blurring of the boundaries of the market as a result of the growing involvement of the institutions of the discount market in the business of the recently established markets for local authority bonds, inter-bank loans and Euro-currencies. Interest rates and market conditions in these markets and in the other markets for short money, like that for government bonds, interact strongly, indeed, the Radcliffe Report suggested that they behaved, in many ways, like one market. Certainly the repercussions from the activities of the monetary authorities in one

[1] The Bank of England has required the ending of this syndicate.

market quickly spread through the others. Furthermore, dealings in short term bonds play such an important part in the business of the discount houses, and there is so much switching of assets between the various types of bills and bonds, that it is difficult not to think of them as one market. Some other firms which share in the market for Treasury bills also handle short bonds, call money, foreign exchange and bullion, and act as intermediaries between the banks and the stock jobbers.

There are eleven major discount houses, all members of the London Discount Market Association. They are:

Alexanders (1891)
Allen Harvey Ross (1946)
Cater Ryder (merged 1960)
Clive Discount (1959)
*Gerrard & Reid (1962)
Gillett Bros (1946)
*[Gerrard & Reid & National Discount merged in 1969]

Jessel Toynbee (1943)
*National Discount (1856)
Smith St Aubyn (1943)
Union Discount (1885)
King & Shaxson (1946)
Seccombe Marshall and Campion (1956)

The dates in brackets show when the houses became registered companies. Apart from the list above there are a small number of firms which play a highly specialized part in the market, e.g. acting as intermediaries between banks and stock jobbers, but the market is largely in the hands of the members of the Association, of which Alexanders, National Discount and Union Discount are much the biggest. While some of the houses have become associates of clearing banks, merchant banks or other banks, they are mostly independent of the great banking concerns. And while they now operate in other markets handling huge sums of money they remain for the most part relatively small institutions with no complex organization and a small number of employees. They are specialists in borrowing for very short and lending for longer but not for long periods. They take up 'surplus' money at a low rate on interest and lend at a slightly higher rate though often the 'jobbing margin' is very small, sometimes as little as one-thirtysecond.

Borrowing in the market

The basic function of the discount houses is to mobilize the funds which are not in use for very short periods of time and to make these funds available for longer periods for the use of government, commerce and industry. These funds are derived in the main from the

Bank of England, the clearing banks and the other banks – merchant, foreign and others.

Table 20. SOURCES OF BORROWED FUNDS (£M.)

	1958	1966	1972	1978
Bank of England	98	82	16	468
Clearing Banks	51	978	910	1545
Scottish Banks	85	94	127	118
Other Deposit Banks	84	11	74	216
Accepting Houses	263	201	949	169
Other lenders	47	119	376	1217
Total	1006	1484	2452	3733

The banks make use of the discount market to get some return on the money which they must have easily available to meet their liabilities if they should be called on to discharge this debt. The funds of this kind which the discount houses borrow from the banks are liable to recall at very short notice. These very short-term funds which make up the working capital of the market can be classified under five headings:

(*a*) privilege money, (*b*) good money, (*c*) overnight money, (*d*) 'last-resort' money, (*e*) short fall money

Privilege money arises from the surplus on the day-to-day business of the banks. After the daily bank clearing there is a settlement of accounts between the banks. Some banks find their cash position worsened, and in order to meet the requirement of an 8 per cent cash to deposits ratio, they will call in these funds from the discount houses and other 'privilege' borrowers. Other banks will find their cash position improved and they will not want the surplus to lie idle even for a short time. They will check their cash position and decide how much they can lend. The discount houses have to balance their books at the end of each day, and they will be looking for funds to replace those which had to be returned to those banks which needed to strengthen their cash position after the clearing. The discount houses will usually be able to obtain funds from other banks so long as 'calling' has been limited to a few banks. If there is a general tightening of credit in the market then they may have to invoke the traditional right to borrow from the Bank of England. There is a marriage of interests between the discount houses looking for funds and the banks wanting to place their money. The rate paid by the

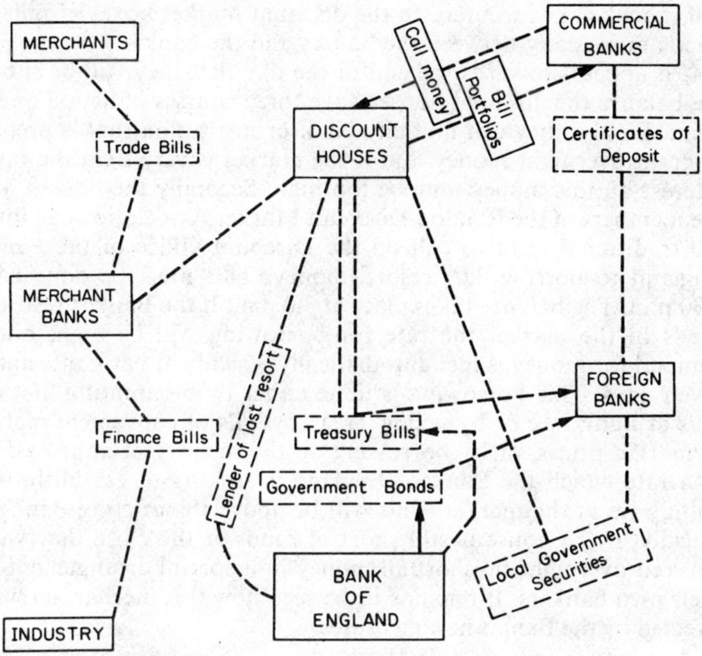

THE DISCOUNT MARKET

banks to depositors is usually not more than 2 per cent less than the prevailing Bank rate. This deposit rate is known as the basic rate. Privilege borrowers pay as little as ½ per cent above this basic rate. Privilege money is naturally very unstable changing hands frequently, perhaps every day, but it does not form a large part of the working capital of the discount market. It averaged about £5 million a day in 1970.

Good money is also liable to quick recall, but in practice it is left by the banks semi-permanently with the discount houses, and only called in exceptional circumstances. Good money earns a rate of interest three-eighths above the basic rate. The clearing banks provide about two-thirds of the funds borrowed by the discount houses and this borrowing has to be secured by bills or bonds in portfolios of suitable maturity, which has to be lodged with the lenders. A distinguishing characteristic of the inter-bank loan market is that the call money is not secured. In the discount market boxes of bills and bonds move daily between the houses and the banks.

If it appears towards the end of the day that they will be short at the balance the discount houses have three courses of action open to them. Firstly, they can find any bank or institution that is prepared to grant overnight money, but if the market is very tight the rate of interest on this money may be too high. Secondly the houses which are members of the London Discount Market Association can invoke the traditional right to call on the Discount Office of the Bank of England to borrow 'last resort' money. This must be done before 2.30 p.m. The balance takes place at 3.0 p.m. If the Bank is restricting funds in the market the rate for borrowing will be high, but the demand for money is met automatically, usually at bank rate and for seven days. This borrowing is done either by discounting first class bills at Bank rate or by selling Treasury bills of convenient maturity at market prices, or by borrowing on the security of approved bills at a rate which the Bank of England is seeking to establish as the going rate in the market. This will be above the existing Bank rate. Thirdly, if the house is still short of funds at the close they will be covered overnight by shortfall money in a special arrangement with their own bankers. It remains to be seen how this mechanism will be affected by the Bank's new measures.

Lending in the Market

The lending function of the discount houses is performed by holding bills, bonds and Negotiable Certificates of Deposit (CDs). The bills are made up of bank bills and trade bills, which together are known as commercial bills, and U.K. Treasury bills. The bonds now include local government securities and other bonds as well as U.K. government bonds. The recently introduced Negotiable Certificates of Deposits which are described later are denominated either in sterling or in dollars. The table of assets below shows how the twelve members of the Discount Market Association distribute their funds now as compared with the distribution in 1958.

Bank bills are commercial bills of exchange which have been accepted by merchant banks, which are usually accepting houses of high financial standing. The trade bills are bills of exchange which arise out of foreign or inland trade transactions. The discount houses make their profit on these bills either by borrowing more cheaply than they lend – this is discounting – or by selling at a higher price than they paid for the bill – this is called jobbing. The margins are usually

Table 21. TABLE OF ASSETS 1958 AND 1973 (July)

Assets in £m	1958	*Assets in £m*	1973
Cash	10	Negotiable CDs*	635
Treasury Bills	594	Treasury Bills	259
Commercial Bills	70	Commercial Bills†	615
Government Stock	321	Government Stock	253
Other Assets	58	Other Assets	201
		Local Authority Bonds	651
	1053		2614

*£120 million of dollar certificates of deposit to be added in.
†Including Local Authority Bills

very narrow but the sums involved are huge. (See p. 64.) The houses earn a discount by buying the bill for less than its face value and then receiving the full value when the bill matures usually in three months time. The size of this margin or discount is determined by (*a*) the credit standing of the firm that is using the bill to borrow money; (*b*) the time the bill has to run to maturity; (*c*) the prevailing rates which the discount has to pay to borrow in the market. This may be illustrated by the following example. On November 28 1969 the average discount on allotment for ninety-one day Treasury bills was just over £7.14*s*.9*d* p.a. so that the discount houses paid about £98.1*s*.1*d*. for a ninety-one day bill which would be worth £100 when it matured in ninety-one days time. This represents a discount rate of 7¾ per cent at a time when the rates the commercial banks charged for call money fluctuated between a basic rate of 6 three-eighths per cent and a peak of 7 five-eighths per cent. If the houses borrowed at the latter rate their margin would have been as little as one-eighth per cent. The margin on commercial bills is higher, partly because the credit standing of the commercial borrower is not as high as that of the Treasury. On November 28 1969 prime Bank bills, i.e. those accepted by houses of the highest standing carried a discount rate of 8¾ per cent, while trade bills, simply raised by traders and therefore of less creditworthiness, carried a higher rate, between 9½ per cent and 9¾ per cent.

The Treasury bill

The discount houses provide the government with working funds by buying bills and bonds. The Treasury bill is at the heart of this credit creation. It is the chief means of Exchequer short term borrowing, though there was a dramatic decline in its importance relative to other forms of borrowing during 1969 and early 1970. Compare the table of pre-war Debt circulation with the table of discount houses assets from 1960–1970:

Table 22. PRE-WAR DEBT CIRCULATION

Financial Year	*Commercial Bills* (£m)	*Treasury Bills* (£m)	*Total* (£m)
1922–23	429	490	919
1927–28	508	502	1010
1932–33	247	571	818
1936–37	276	580	856

Table 23. DISCOUNT HOUSES ASSETS 1960–78

Year	*Commercial Bills*		*Treasury Bills*		*Government Bonds*		*Total*
	£m	%	£m	%	£m	%	£m
1960	117	10	574	48	440	37	1085
1963	249	19	529	41	442	34	1305
1965	339	23	484	33	500	34	1455
1968	560	34	471	28	306	18	1663
1970	697	30	876	37	160	7	2352
1974	1182	42	564·5	19	13	0·5	2821
1978	1202	31	402	10	526	13	3906

Source: *B.E.Q.B.*

There are seasonal swings in the issue of Treasury bills and in March 1970 the issue of these bills reached the low figure of £80 million a week, the lowest in post-war years. Discount house holdings were down to less than £200 millions. The highest point reached in the holdings of government bonds since the war was in March 1967 (£678 million). Treasury bills are issued each week for ninety-one days and in various denominations, the newest of which, for £250,000 appeared first in April 1968 when different colouring for each denomination was also introduced to facilitate counting and sorting. 'Tap' Treasury bills are those which are issued directly to government departments and do not come to the market in great quantities. Market Treasury bills are offered to tender each week and apart from the institutions already said to be part of the market, other tenderers, through the Bank of England and the discount houses, are the overseas holders of sterling, and domestic lenders, which includes those companies which have short term cash surpluses. The London Discount Market Association traditionally covers the tender each week but the number of bills which the market actually takes depends upon the competition of the other institutions in the market.

Summary:

Treasury bills issued
- (a) by tender
- (b) through the 'tap'
  - (i) to government departments
    Savings bank
    Statutory Insurance Funds
    Exchange Equalization Account
  - (ii) to certain overseas monetary authorities

Tender Issue to
- (a) Discount houses syndicate*
- (b) Banks, including foreign banks
- (c) Brokers

* This syndicate has been abolished in the 1971 measures

It is by varying the issue of Treasury bills and by managing the volume of bills outstanding through open market operations that the Bank of England maintains much of its control of the money market. The growing leakage of bills to non-bank institutions weakens this Bank of England control. The bills are issued by the Bank as part of its function of managing the National Debt. That part of the government's financial requirements that cannot be met by longer term borrowing must be covered by the Treasury bill issue. It is sometimes difficult for the Bank of England to reconcile the conflicting aims of control of the volume of credit in the money market and the management of the Debt. A rise in interest rates manipulated by the Bank of England to tighten credit in the money market inevitably causes an increase in the cost of borrowing for the government. If a shortage of funds prompts an increase in the issue of Treasury bills to the market the authorities' control over the creation of credit by the banks is weakened. This is because market Treasury bills, when held by the clearing banks, are liquid assets. An increase in the volume of liquid assets increases the banks' powers of credit creation.

We can now see that the Treasury bill is of major importance in the short term money market because it is the instrument by which the funds of the banks and certain non-bank institutions, which have to be readily available at short notice, are put at the disposal of the government, where it is not possible or preferable to raise longer term funds. The discount houses are the foremost institutions in the market for Treasury bills and act as intermediaries between the clearing banks and the Bank of England. The banks do not tender directly but buy their bills at various stages of maturity, usually not less than seven days old, from the discount houses. In this way they are able to adjust their liquidity position by having a suitable volume of bills maturing at the times when they expect to need cash. The return the banks receive on these bills will be greater the longer the period they hold the bills. In this way they attempt to satisfy the conflicting aims of liquidity and profitability for their assets.

Abolish the discount houses?

It has been argued that the role of the discount houses as intermediaries in the market for Treasury bills is unnecessary and an expensive anachronism. The morning ritual of top-hatted brokers from the discount houses visiting the banks continues even though most of the business is done by phone. The Bank of England provides cash to enable the discount houses to take up Treasury bills even when money is tight. In this way it is lending to the market so that the market in turn can lend it to the Exchequer. Why does the Bank of England not lend direct to the Exchequer? Brian Griffiths in *Competition in Banking* has recently added his criticism to that of numerous other writers on the matter of the 'syndicated bid' by the twelve discount houses, who all tender at this price. Sayers points out that 'every discount house finds that its allotment bears the same proportion to its tender, sometimes a high proportion, sometimes a low one, according to whether the outside tenders [at the cheaper rate] are small or large'. It is surely a restrictive practice and there is probably some monopoly profit.

The discount houses defend their practices with several telling arguments. They point out that by operating through the market instead of lending directly to the Exchequer the Bank of England is able to exercise control over the conditions of the money market and particularly over short term interest rates. They believe that the discount houses are in direct competition with other institutions at the tender for Treasury bills. They are also dependent for their funds on the clearing banks who are quick to squeeze them if their profit margins become too large. They perform the valuable function of setting a rate in the market by deciding what changes in interest rates are likely during the ninety-one day life of the Treasury bill. The stability of prices in the market would be much less without this lead. Again, it is an advantage to the government to be sure that its cash requirements will be met because the houses underwrite the whole of the Treasury bill tender each week. The banks support the continued existence of the discount houses because they are provided with a ready means of earning interest on their very short term funds and facilities for quickly rearranging the liquidity of their assets, i.e. adjusting their cash position. The Radcliffe Committee concluded 'that the importance of the work of the discount houses in relation to Treasury bills lies not in any indispensibility . . . but rather in the fact that they make a highly efficient market in instruments which are very convenient to the Exchequer'.

The commercial bill

There have been changes in the relative importance of the different types of bills in the business of the discount houses. The resurgence of the commercial bill in recent years reflects the adaptability of this credit instrument and the versatility of the discount houses in their use of it. The legal definition of the commercial bill of exchange gives some indication of the wide range of uses to which this instrument could be adapted. It is 'an unconditional order in writing, addressed by one person to another, signed by the person giving it, requiring the person to whom it is addressed to pay on demand or at a fixed or determinable future time a sum certain in money to or to the order of a specified person or to bearer'. The make-up of a 'bank' commercial bill of exchange is shown over.

The commercial bill is a credit instrument because when the person to whom it is addressed, the drawee, signs it, he becomes the acceptor, and he creates credit in so far as he has in this way given a 'promise to pay'. If the bill is to be acceptable to other people it must be accepted (endorsed) by a recognized bank known to have the credit standing necessary to guarantee the bill. By accepting the bill the bank (accepting house) does not give the funds to the drawer but merely lends its 'good name' which makes the bill into a readily negotiable instrument, i.e. financial institutions are prepared to buy it because eventual payment is guaranteed by the acceptor. Discount houses and clearing banks are ready to buy bills (known as bank bills) which have been endorsed by a recognized accepting house. The acceptor receives a commission for lending its name to the bill, and, of course, for taking the risk that in the event of default when the bill is presented for payment they will have to find the sum

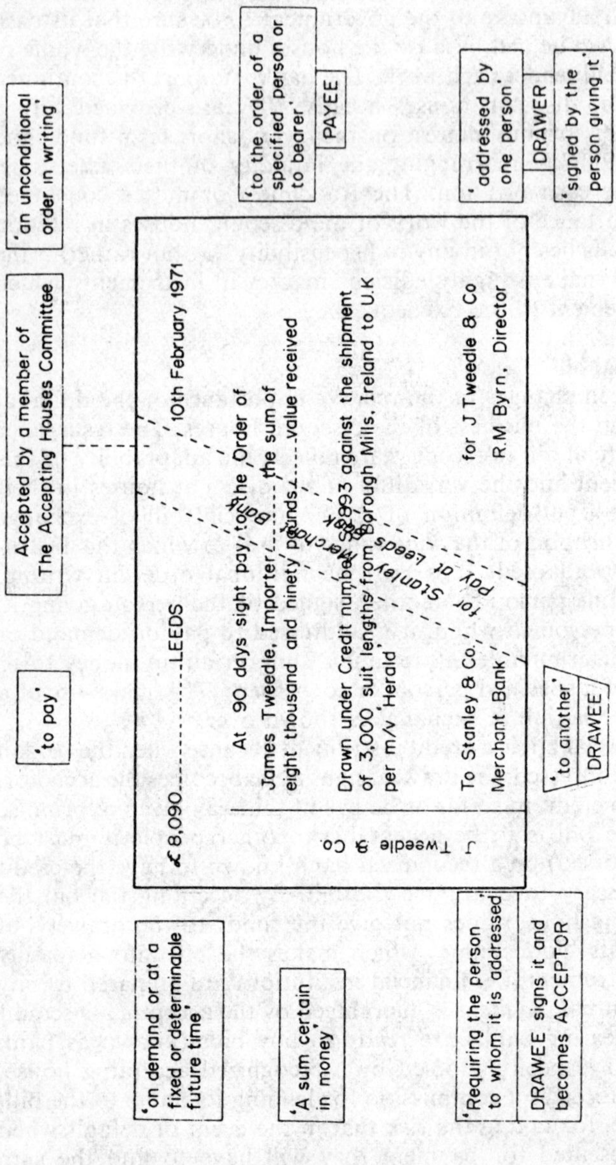

Freely adapted from 'The Bill on London' *Gillett Bros.*

involved. Some bills are accepted by clearing banks and others by foreign banks in London, but by far the largest number are handled by the eighteen foremost accepting houses who are represented on the Accepting Houses Committee. These accepting houses are also merchant banks.

The bills accepted by these houses carry the finest rates of any of the commercial bills on the market. These interest or discount rates are determined by the credit standing of the acceptor, the amount of outstanding credit which the drawer already has with the acceptor, the length of time the bill has to run, and the prevailing conditions in the discount market. The discount houses have a limit on the amount of bills which they are prepared to buy from any one accepting house. While the rates on bank bills are very fine they are higher than for Treasury bills for time and expertise has to be taken up by the acceptor, and later by the buyers, to ascertain the credit worthiness of the other parties involved. It is the buyer of the bill, i.e. the discount house or the bank, which lends money at a discount – buying the bill for less than its face value and receiving the full value when the bill matures. The holder may choose to sell the bill before that time in order to increase the liquidity of his assets (i.e. raise more cash). In this case the holder would still receive more than he paid for it but less than the face value depending on how long the bill still has to run. Each day the bill becomes a little more valuable.

Some bills do not carry the name of a recognized bank. They are simply accepted by the trader who is buying the goods and are drawn on the traders who are supplying the goods. If the acceptor's credit standing is well enough known the bill is marketable, but requires a higher rate of interest (discount) to compensate for the extra risk involved. If the acceptor is unable to pay on the maturity date the holder has no recourse to the drawer.

The function of the commercial bill is to provide the seller (drawer) with immediate funds instead of him having to wait three months or more for payment for the goods he has sold. For this privilege he pays the current rate of discount. 'Sight drafts' are not instruments of credit because they are payable by the acceptor on presentation. Promisory notes must be distinguished from bills of exchange because they are not immediately negotiable.

The Bank of England takes an interest in the business of accepting commercial bills and grants a special privilege, reviewed annually, to the houses in the Accepting Houses Committee. The privilege is that the bills which they accept can be rediscounted at the Bank of

England. This is a method of borrowing in the last resort. If the holder of these 'eligible' bills present them to the Bank they will be rediscounted at bank rate. In recent years good trade bills have come to be offered to the Bank as eligible instruments and this has been a factor in enhancing their importance.

Newer credit instruments

The discount houses have shown a capacity to adapt their business so as to make the most profitable use of the various types of credit instruments according to their availability on the market. They have recently begun to deal in Negotiable Certificates of Deposit. These were first introduced in New York in 1961 by bankers who wished to meet a rise in demand for advances when there was no comparable rise in deposits. The way to attract more money is to offer a higher rate of interest, but they did not want to raise interest rates generally. The certificate is exchanged for a fixed deposit and the holders can redeem this deposit before maturity by selling it to a third party. It is negotiable by law. In this way the banks were able to compete for deposits by offering CDs at favourable rates of interest (discount) without bringing about a general rise in interest rates. Only five houses deal in dollar certificates because of a Bank of England ruling which will not allow a house to run a dollar book and be associated with a foreign currency broker. From October 1968 banks in the U.K. were authorized to issue sterling CDs. Their minimum denomination is £50,000 and their life varies from three months to five years. By the end of 1970 the discount houses held almost £300 million of sterling CDs and were the major holders of this type of money, though the accepting houses and clearing banks are also holders. CDs have attracted to the market funds previously invested elsewhere. This is welcomed by the discount houses as a counter to developments which are tending to reduce idle balances. The growth of the well organized inter-bank market in which the merchant banks and foreign banks are leading operators has resulted in funds which would formerly have been available to the discount houses by-passing the market. It was their concern about the effects of the development of new markets on the sources of their finance along with the relative stagnation of their traditional bill business in the first half of the 1960s which spurred the discount houses to look for new lines. Apart from the dealings in certificates of deposit the discount houses have taken an interest in the market for local authority securities and other sterling bills, which include the Treasury bills of the Northern

Ireland Government and local authority bills (as well commercial bills).

Table 24. DISCOUNT HOUSES HOLDINGS OF CDS

£m	1967	1968	1970	1971	1972	May 1973
$ CDs	14	39	39	108	134	120
£ CDs	—	56	268	457	420	616

Table 25. DISCOUNT HOUSES HOLDINGS OF LOCAL AUTHORITY SECURITIES

	1966	1968	1970	1972	May 1973
Securities (£m)	101	148	224	529	526

Table 26. DISCOUNT HOUSES HOLDINGS OF OTHER STERLING BILLS

	1966	1968	1970	1972	May 1973
Other bills (£m)	404	560	697	574	510

Some of the houses have a small business in foreign currency acceptances, though they keep this business apart from their sterling activities. Sterling money broking is another recent development, and some houses continue a small interest in the equity market, sometimes through broking concerns in which they have acquired interests. All this is ample evidence that the market was ready for change and that the discount houses were interested in new ideas for business and able to demonstrate their adaptability.

The resurgence of the commercial bill

However interesting and important the development of new fringe activities of the discount houses may seem it should be remembered that the traditional bill and bond business is still the bread and butter work and that opportunities for considerable profits are possible in this business. The discount market had originally grown up to deal with the discounting of commercial bills and from Table 22 it can be seen that in the 1920s the commercial bill was holding its own with the Treasury bill. The decline of the commercial bill in the 1930s was an inevitable consequence of the general decline of trade and business at that time. By the end of the Second World War the commercial bill business had so declined and the Treasury bill and government bond business so expanded that the discount market had changed fundamentally from being an institutional adjunct of the finance of foreign trade to become an appendage of the banking system and of

National Debt administration. Even by the mid-1950s the demise of the commercial bill seemed but a matter of time.

Table 27 DISCOUNT HOUSES ASSETS 1955–60

	Commercial Bills		*Treasury Bills*		*Government Bonds*	
	£m	%	£m	%	£m	%
1955	45	4	652	61	307	29
1958	70	7	594	56	321	31
1960	117	10	574	48	440	37

Sources: *MBR* and *BEQB*

The 1960s saw a remarkable resurgence of the commercial bill (see Table 23). The discount market had been built on dealings in the bill by brokers who acted as intermediaries finding credit for merchants trading in different parts of the world. Some merchants wanted credit extended to them on the security of the goods they were shipping. Others who lived in industrial areas wanted to borrow through bills from the banks in rural areas which had surplus funds. The resurgence of the commercial bill has been not so much a revival of these traditional functions as the adapting of the bill to new uses. The imaginative dealers in the discount market recognized the flexibility of the instruments and institutions of the market as suppliers of credit. While the traditional trade bill continued to decline the finance bill, entirely an instrument of short-term credit, enjoyed a considerable growth. The finance bill could be defined as a commercial bill which involves no exchange of goods but simply a promise to pay a certain sum of money on a given date. The bills could be drawn against stocks of goods in a warehouse. They may be drawn by finance companies and accepted by merchant banks.

There are a number of reasons why this business expanded so rapidly at this time. Bill brokers realized that bill finance was becoming increasingly competitive with other forms of short-term credit, and particularly the bank overdraft. This was partly the result of acceptance commissions being forced down by the activities of the foreign banks, and partly the result of the abolition of the *ad valorum* stamp duty in 1961. Large industrial and commercial concerns were becoming increasingly interested in finding ways around the restrictions on lending which were being applied to the clearing banks. Many large companies began to draw bills at this time in order to provide working capital. The finance companies which specialized in hire-purchase finance were also actively interested. Another reason for the lively interest in these bills was that business in the main instrument of the market, the Treasury bill, had begun to decline. The main reason for this was the fall in the deficit in the public sector. But the gradual swing to government bonds as the main means of supplying Exchequer requirements was another important factor. The restrictive credit policy encouraged the authorities to cut down on the issue of Treasury bills. The discount houses were becoming less enamoured of the business particularly after their experiences at the time of devaluation in the autumn of 1967. Angus Oldaker of Gerrard and Reid described the situation in the *Times Annual Financial and Economic Review* in this way: 'Treasury bill offers were increasing in size, and as there were few other takers discount houses had to accept, because of their undertaking to cover the tender, an unwonted (and unwanted) allocation of paper which was inevitably to lead, as events transpired, to very heavy losses. Houses had to cope with considerable increased offerings of bank bills, and short of refusing traditional business of this kind altogether, had no option but to accept the losses involved, protecting themselves as best they could by continually raising their rates.' Discount houses tend to make losses on their Treasury bill business when Bank rate is raised and profits when the Bank rate is lowered. The rate at which they tender for Treasury bills is determined by their own borrowing costs, and by the rate of discount which they think they can obtain in the face of competitive tenders from other institutions.

During the 1960s therefore the discount houses were rearranging the holding of their assets so as to take advantage of changes in the profitability and availability of the different types of paper they deal in. From 1955 to early 1968 there was a growth of business in government bonds which paralleled the decline in the Treasury bill business. The houses deal in short bonds originally issued for the Exchequer with a life of from one to five years, and in long bonds which have lived most of their life and are approaching maturity. These bonds carry fixed interest rates and therefore yield a positive return over the rates at which the houses can borrow. But because houses often have to sell bonds before they mature the price of the bonds is an import factor in the profitability of the business. If interest rates rise the price of the bonds falls. (Alan Day explains this very well in *Economics of Money*.) In order to avoid serious losses which might result from a sudden fall in bond prices the houses have tended to limit their holdings of this paper. But the discount houses do help to provide an efficient market which is essential if changes in interest rates are to be effective, as without such a market buying and selling would be hindered. Interest rates must be free to move if the discount houses are to have the opportunity of making good margins on their bill and bond business. The authorities' borrowing policy is an important influence on the market. While they were shifting their influence from Treasury bills to government bonds in the years up to 1968, the total of this borrowing was fluctuating around £1,000 million. Since 1968 the government has been enjoying a surplus and this has brought a significant fall in its borrowing requirements. Total government borrowing in the discount market is now around the £700 million mark. In 1970 there has been something of a swing back from bonds to Treasury bills. It is as well for the discount houses that their business in commercial and other sterling bills, local authority securities, sterling CDs, and other lines is continuing to grow. The status of good trade bills has been enhanced and their future prospects improved by the recognition of their 'eligibility' by the Bank of England, but the easing of credit restrictions in the banking sector and the measures of 1971 are likely to erode their position.

What is the position of the discount houses today?

1. Their existence depends on the favourable attitude of other financial institutions, and particularly the clearing banks and the Bank of England. The houses must be able to obtain their funds from the banks, and the banks must continue to obtain their bills through the houses. The authorities must continue to service the Debt by the issue of bills and bonds as they have done in the past, and give their recognition to certain bills for eligibility as collateral for last resort lending. They must allow the free movement of interest rates. It is reported that the clearing banks regard the discount houses as institutions conveniencing them through the outlet they provide for call loans and also performing certain financial services which they themselves have no ambition to provide. Of the Bank of England's attitude to the discount houses Leslie O'Brien in evidence to the Radcliffe Committee said the survival of the discount market 'may not be entirely due to the fact that the clearing banks like it so much. It may be because the Bank of England likes it also. We believe it to be the most flexible mechanism for looking after the needs for short term money that there is in the world'.

2. The justification of the market is its efficiency in mobilising idle balances and other very short term money for lending to industry, trade and the government. It has been able to demonstrate the adapt-

ability of its institutions and instruments in channelling-in funds from previously untapped sources.

3. The authorities also find the market provides a delicate mechanism for controlling short term interest rates and a means of making Bank rate more effective. It helps to even out unwanted fluctuations of bill and bond prices and interest changes. The Bank of England further recognized the importance of the market in the supply of short term credit by bringing the houses within the ambit of its directives on credit restriction in a letter in 1965.

4. While many criticisms have been levelled at the discount market in the past and in the present most critics can see no sudden end to its activities. Scammell concludes 'only a great upheaval in the financial system and a great exercise in a priori financial planning would bring about the discount market's elimination, and for great a priori plans, particularly in the financial field the British have neither enthusiasm nor genius'.

5. From September 1971 the discount houses were required to maintain a 50 per cent public sector lending ratio, and this coupled with a reluctance to hold relatively long-term assets at a time when interest rates were rising explains why their business in CDs has not continued to expand. However this requirement produced undesirable by-products which made management of the market for government debt more difficult. In July 1973 therefore the public sector lending ratio was replaced by 'a control which limits aggregate holdings of certain assets by each house to a maximum of twenty times its capital and reserves. These are all assets other than those defined as public sector assets for the purpose of the discarded 50% ratio.'[1] These defined assets are:

Balances at the Bank of England
U.K. and Northern Ireland Treasury bills
British government stocks } with not more than five years to
Local authority stocks } maturity
Eligible local authority and other bills
Local authority negotiable bonds
Nationalized Industries Bank bills.

The authorities are confident that the 'twenty times multiplied' will not weaken their influence over control of credit while it will give the discount houses greater flexibility in managing their books.

6. The new arrangements encouraged the banks to increase their total lending to the discount market since it qualified as a reserve asset.

[1] See *B.E.Q.B.*, September 1973

4.
THE MERCHANT BANKS

In a previous chapter we have seen that various titles are given to the banks with numerous branches throughout the country which specialize in handling our deposits and making short-term advances. Those that enjoy the facilities of the London Clearing House are known as the clearing banks, and these are dominated by the 'Big Four' – Barclays, Lloyds, Midland and National Westminster. These banks are otherwise known as commercial banks, deposit banks and joint stock banks.

Various names are also used to describe the merchant banks, but care has to be taken in using these terms as they do not embrace all the same institutions. Just as there are some deposit banks which are not clearing banks so there are some merchant banks which cannot properly be called accepting houses, or issuing houses. The accepting houses are those merchant banks which handle acceptance credits, and the foremost sixteen are members of the Accepting Houses Committee. The fifty or so merchant banks which have issuing of securities as part of their business are mostly members of the Issuing Houses Committee. It should be realized, though, that institutions other than merchant banks take part in the new issue business.

The important thing for the reader to appreciate is the considerable variety of institutions which have assumed the title merchant bank, and there are few books dealing with these institutions which do not go on to say that many of them are neither merchants nor banks. However the origins of most of the leading institutions using this name are connected with the financing of trade and commerce. Listed below are the sixteen members of the Accepting Houses Committee with the date of their foundation.

Barings – 1772	Arbuthnot Latham – 1833
Rothschilds – 1804	Guiness Mahon – 1836
Schroder Wagg – 1804	Morgan Grenfell – 1838
Brandt's – 1805	Hambros – 1839
Antony Gibbs – 1808	Kleinwort Benson – 1830
Brown Shipley – 1810	Hill Samuel – 1831

Samuel Montagu – 1853	Lazard – 1877
Warburg – 1864	Charterhouse Japhet – 1893

The list contains some of the famous household names of the financial world, and there is no doubt that some of these institutions have enjoyed, and still do enjoy, an enormous prestige and mystique which far outweighs their actual financial strength. In the nineteenth century some were capable of making or breaking governments in some parts of the world, and it was to these houses that the British Government turned for advice on a whole range of international questions that were often not financial. They were the glamorous institutions of the financial world, and though an aura of secrecy surrounded much of their business, and their London offices were rather anonymous places, their names, and those of their principals, featured prominently in many of the important financial deals of the nineteenth and twentieth centuries.

Acceptances

The acceptance credit business has been the bread and butter work of the acceptance houses for most of their lives. This business has been described in some detail in the chapter on the discount houses but it is worth developing the discussion a little further. The accepting house lends its name to a commercial bill to give the drawer of the bill, and anyone who discounts the bill for him, a guarantee that they will receive its face value when the bill matures. The house which is discounting the bill may never have heard of the drawer of the bill but he will be prepared to hold it because it is guaranteed by a well-known bank or accepting house. The bills accepted by London banks and accepting houses of undoubted standing command the finest rates of discount and therefore provide the cheapest form of borrowing on this instrument. The 'quality' of the bill thus affects the cost of borrowing. Bills carrying the name of the leading accepting houses are recognized by the Bank of England as being eligible for collateral in the last resort lending. In return the accepting houses must make strenuous efforts to maintain their financial soundness in the eyes of the Bank. Before the house will lend its name to a bill it will ascertain the credit-worthiness of the drawer. Over many years merchant banks have acquired a good deal of knowledge of their clientele. Where foreign parties unknown to the London merchant bank are involved the bank might prefer to use Reimbursement Credits whereby a foreign bank will guarantee the bill before credit is granted. It is the high rates for short term credit in continental countries and the operation of credit restriction which has boosted the business which merchant banks have done for foreign parties. It was the search in the world money markets for funds to finance the business of international lending through bills which uncovered the funds which gave rise to the Euro-currency business.

The sixteen members of the Accepting Houses Committee dominate the acceptance credit business. Of the £813 million of acceptances outstanding held by all institutions in the U.K. in 1970 the sixteen houses held some £329 million. The revival of the bill has been an important factor in the profit earnings of the houses; e.g. in 1964 Hambros earned £44 million on acceptances, their largest single profit earner; and in the same year Kleinwort Benson's acceptances brought in £24 million. But in fact the growth of this line of business has not kept pace with the profits earned from the other business of the merchant banks in the 1960s. Holdings of acceptance credits increased to only £342 million by the beginning of 1971 from £136 million in 1960, while advances went up from £155 million in 1960 to £1,164 million in 1970. Current and deposit accounts went from £334 million in 1960 to £2,514 million in 1970.

New issues

There are nearly sixty members of the Issuing Houses Committee and most of these institutions describe themselves as merchant banks, though there are some other institutions which handle new issues. The object of the Issuing Houses Committee is 'to act as a consultative and advisory body representing the interests of banking houses and other institutions in respect of their activities as issuing houses, and in particular to provide a medium for placing before the government, the Bank of England, the Council of the Stock Exchange and other public bodies, authorities and individuals the views of the association on matters affecting such activities'.[1] The Association was formed in 1945 and had as its first Chairman Lionel Fraser of Helbert Wagg. Its offices and secretariat which it shares with the Accepting Houses Committee are housed in the Kleinwort Benson Building.

The issuing houses help their clients in a number of ways. Their basic function is to help find new capital for companies wishing to expand. They seldom lend the capital themselves for their business is to put those who wish to borrow in touch with those who have

[1] Central Office of Information pamphlet 24.

funds to lend. Firms will be advised by their merchant bank as to the best way to raise their capital. The bank will prepare the prospectus for them and arrange for a stock exchange quotation if the firm is going public or is already a public company. It will handle the applications for a new share issue and decide on the allocation if the issue is over-subscribed. If the bank performs all the functions of the issue i.e. broking, underwriting etc., it might receive as much as 2·5 per cent of the value of the issue, but it might well allow other specialists to perform some of the functions. In some cases the issuing house may itself purchase the whole issue and then arrange the sales itself. Apart from these *offers for sale* there is also a method of issue where *offers by tender* are asked for and bids accepted at or above a given price. The merchant bank will also help its clients to make *Rights Issues* to their existing equity holders, and arrange for existing securities to be *listed* even when no new capital is being raised. The banks have the 'know-how to make arrangements with the institutional investors like insurance companies and pension funds. They can even help when it comes to unquoted issues for if a smaller issue bears the name of one of the well-known houses the yield expected by the buyers (to compensate for the risk) will be reduced. Overseas firms or governments making issues in London will receive similar service for their debenture stock or bond issues. The issuing houses also act as registrars for companies and overseas institutions and governments, keeping a record of securities and holders and arranging for payments of dividends.

Financial advice

The merchant banks develop a special banker's relationship with the client firms, and they give advice on all manner of company problems. They like to think of themselves as doctors or specialists in the world of company finance, and give opinions on the presentation of accounts and what dividends should be paid. It is their job to help their clients to make the best use of their assets. As expert readers of the balance sheet they suggest ways in which organization and management could be improved. However the aspect of this function of the merchant banks which most frequently hits the headlines and catches the imagination of the public is their involvement in company mergers, amalgamations and take-overs. Since the mid-1950s there has been a spate of activity in this field as firms have striven to increase their size to take advantage of the economies which result, to increase their competitive strength and to further their prestige – to name but some of the reasons. The merchant banks have had an important part to play in all this. Their responsibility is to their client firm which may either be the one defending its position against the merger or the one trying to carry it through. Whichever the case the merchant bank has to advise on the best tactics to be adopted. In recent years they have worked out new and effective ways of countering unsought bids, but they also have a responsibility to tell the directors when to advise share-holders to accept a bid. A number of take-over incidents rocked the City in the late 1950s. The tactics adopted by the dynamic Warburg house in the British Aluminium affair, in winning the take-over battle for its clients was one of the incidents which led to the setting up of the Take-over Panel on which the I.H.C. and the A.H.C. are represented. A strengthened take-over code was brought out and the Panel reconstituted and given added powers in 1969.

The expansion of the financial advisory side of merchant banking has been the main development of the last decade and it has had its impact on the banks' approach to business. This has become much more competitive. The banks are constantly on the look for new profit areas. There is little similarity between the present-day merchant bankers and those of twenty years ago. The family partners are making way for the professional directors and managers. The all-rounder is being replaced by the specialist heading a streamlined departmentalized organization. The wise septuagenarian is now a much less common figure than the thrusting young executive in his early forties. In this way much of the mystique of the banks has evaporated and the bankers have become much more like their clients, the executives of large companies. With the change of emphasis from credit to advice the bankers' relationship with their clients has also changed. No longer are the firms coming 'cap-in-hand' but they are demanding a wide range of services, and if they are not satisfied with the service they are getting from their bank they are much more prepared than in the past to move to a bank offering a better service. The banks are faced with the problem of how to keep up with the required diversification of services and how to take advantage of the wide range of domestic and international profit opportunities without becoming so large that the essentially personal relationship with their clients is lost.

Investment management

A further important and rapidly expanding function of the merchant banks is that of investment management and advice. The portfolios managed by the leading merchant banks have a value of more than £2,000 million and they have a considerable influence on at least another £1,000 million of investments. But the real power of the merchant banks in the capital market is to be found not so much in the considerable size of the investments they manage or control as in their wide network of clients and contacts throughout the domestic and international markets. Naturally the merchant banks depend on their domestic business to give them a firm foundation on which to launch their international ventures, and the most successful banks in international markets are those with a thriving business at home. Participation by the banks in these international markets takes a variety of forms. At the most direct level we have already seen that the London merchant banks give advice to foreign governments and firms on issues of securities in London, and even in 1964 some £115 million was raised by foreign governments through London. They will also handle the issues and act as registrars and paying agents. The banks provide a full investment advisory service, which is available both to foreign clients wishing to invest in Britain and to British clients wishing to invest abroad. In the past they have been free from competition from the clearing banks in this field. The clearing banks have steered clear after losing an action brought by a customer against Martins Bank for bad advice. They are now reconsidering their position for the returns to investment management in a period when institutional saving has been a major growth field are considerable. The merchant banks have been frequently adapting their investment organization to take advantage of social and economic changes in investment patterns.

Co-operation and consortia

The merchant banks traditionally employed an intricate system of alliances with banks in other countries to facilitate their operations in these countries. Hambros have operated through Laidlaw, their associates in the U.S., while Warburgs had a close association with Kuhn Loeb until it opened its own office in New York. Harriman Reply of New York is partly owned by Philip Hill. Many of these alliances continue to the present, but at a time when their international business is expanding so rapidly, and competition from other institutions is increasing, the merchant banks have felt the need for further, perhaps more direct, links with these countries. As a result seven of the banks have opened offices in such other major financial centres as New York, Paris and Switzerland. Schroders were first into America in the 1920s and by the 1960s its American company was earning more than the home company. Another method of strengthening contacts has been the establishment of subsidiary firms sometimes wholly owned by the merchant bank in this country and sometimes in partnership with one or more other banks. Apart from establishing subsidiaries overseas the merchant banks have cooperated in setting up multi-national banks in a number of countries. Some of these are listed below:

Multi-national Bank	*British Bank involved*	*Established*
Midland & International (Maibl)	Midland	1964
International Commercial	Nat. Westminster	1967
Continental Banking Services	Barclays, Bolsa, Lloyds	1968
Western American	Hambros	1968
Atlantic International	Charterhouse Japhet	1969
Rothschild Intercontinental	Rothschild	1969
Manufacturers Hanover	Rothschild	1969

The growth of multi-national industrial corporations called for banks with similar multi-national link-ups to meet their needs. The services offered by these banks have to be good for large companies have, in some cases, established their own finance departments with a brief to gain access to the money markets of the world and handle their own foreign currency transactions. Moreover the large American banks are very active in this area. The banks have been active in arranging consortia to meet the huge financial requirements of multinational firms or foreign governments.

The Economist Supplement on Banking highlighted the difficulty the merchant banks have in making the right decision of how to develop their links overseas. In the 1969 supplement they commented: 'London's merchant banks are rethinking the question of whether they need overseas offices, especially in New York. If they link themselves on an informal basis with banks in the host country they are in danger of having just a visiting card relationship, with little business flowing either way. If they take on a minority stake with another bank, or banks, in the host country, they may limit their freedom to cooperate with all banks. If, on the other hand, they set up their own office in competition with local banks, there is just a danger they may lose whatever benefits arise from having a visiting card or a partner.'

The merchant banks have been very conscious of Britain's move towards Europe. Many of them already have one or more footholds in Europe of the kind described above, but there is still room for an imaginative expansion of banking services to exploit the freedom offered by the Common Market, where a company will be able to raise funds wherever it chooses among the member countries. As yet there is no real European Investment Market, and the European Investment Bank is not fully developed. In 1969 some British nationalized industries and public utilities raised more than £80 million in Europe. While Western European borrowers raised more then £1,200 million through foreign and international bond issues. The 1960s also saw the development of the Euro-bond market.

The merchants banks play their part in the recently developed secondary money markets. The markets for Euro-currencies, local authority bills, inter-company funds, inter-bank funds and certificates of deposit have all enjoyed a remarkable growth in recent years. Their role is sometimes that of a money-broker, sometimes an advisory one, and sometimes that of full participants in the borrowing and lending business of the market. The sums dealt in are seldom less than £$\frac{1}{4}$ million, and the total marketable debt of the local authorities alone is more than £17,000 million, while the funds of the Euro-currency market probably amount to £20,000 million.

Apart from these main lines of activity some merchant banks perform a number of other important tasks. They are among the 180 or so foreign exchange dealers authorized by the Bank of England. This business grew out of the handling of foreign bills and is of course essential to active dealing in the international money markets. The merchant banks dominate the London Gold Market (see Chap. 5) and meetings to fix the price take place in the House of Rothschild. Bullion and foreign exchange dealings are perhaps the most obvious merchant functions remaining to the merchant banks though some banks do occasionally arrange for the shipping of commodities. They do however have interests in a wide range of business activities e.g. Samuels in shipping, especially oil tankers, Brown Shipley in the wholesale supply of foreign banknotes; others have continued their interest in insurance problems connected with the shipping of goods and the financing of trade. Ventures as different as holiday camps in the Mediterranean and North Sea gas have attracted the banks, and they have arranged medium and even long-term finance for such projects. Flemings, the largest single manager of investment funds controlling some £600 million have a successful record of unit trust management, and once raised £60 million for British Petroleum. Some banks have taken up factoring, the administering of clients' debts, even taking over the entire business of billing and collecting the debts. Leopold Joseph have become one of the leading names in the City for trading in 'investment dollars' which are the medium through which British investors can purchase securities or other assets outside the sterling area. All this amply illustrates the theme of diversification which runs through the history of the merchant banks in the 1960s. These diverse services earned £11 million in invisible items in 1965. Even in 1959 the Radcliffe Committee wrote of the merchant banks and accepting houses: 'In fact the business of the accepting houses is not standardized or homogeneous. Each house has its own characteristics and specialities on which it is regarded as an authority, but the granting of acceptance credits to finance the trade of others is a business which they all have in common.'

Competition

We have already noted the considerable increase in competition between the merchant banks, but they have also to face growing competition in their main lines of business from outside their ranks. The most formidable operators are the American banks, many of which have been attracted to London by the large Euro-dollar business. In 1968–1969 twelve new American banks opened in the City bringing the total of foreign banks and offices to more than 150. They employ more than 9,000 staff many of them attracted from the London merchant banks. The total deposits of the American banks amount to more than £10,000 million, and the deposits of the other foreign banks to another £2,000 million. They have declared no immediate plans to step up competition for sterling deposits for their main business at the present is in foreign currency deposits, but they are acutely aware of the growing internationalism in banking, a development which explains their presence in London. The London merchant banks face the Americans in all facets of the business of international finance and they have responded to the challenge in a number of different ways. Samuels have linked up with the First New York City Bank raising some £1·8 million by selling them a 15 per cent block of their shares. Others have stressed the personal attention which only they, as small banks, can give to their customers affairs. They concentrate on giving a better guarantee of security and

Bank Deposits 1965 and May 1971

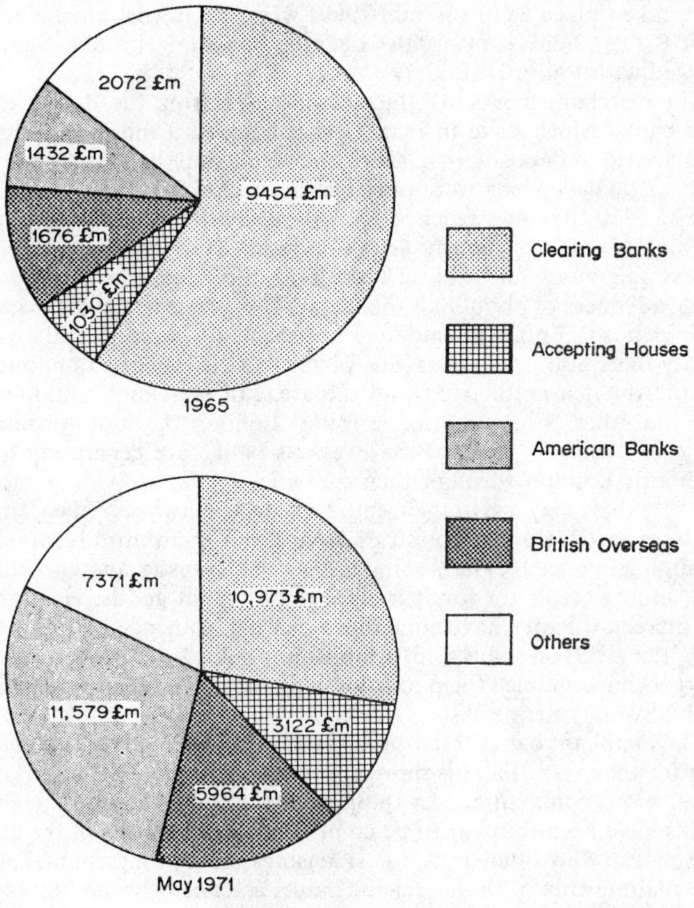

Note: See Table 38 for Bank Deposits 1974–78

liquidity than the foreign banks. Clearly they could not unilaterally match the massive lending power of the American banks but the complicated web of link-ups and consortia usually enable them to overcome this disadvantage. However some banks have been taking more direct action and a number of mergers between merchant banks have taken place as in the mid-1960s when Kleinwort amalgamated with Robert Benson Lonsdale, Lazards bought Stein, and Samuels merged with Philip Hill.

The merchant banks also face competition from the British overseas banks which have in recent years enjoyed a much more spectacular rise in deposits than the London clearing banks. At the end of 1967 their deposits were only just over £2,000 million but by the end of 1970 they had reached £5,500 million from which they were making advances of nearly £3,000 million. Compared with this the accepting houses had only £3,000 million of deposits in 1970 and made advances of about half that total. The overseas banks have won their deposits by an imaginative approach to banking and by the ability to exploit good ideas. Such banks as the Bank of London and South America are active in all the areas of merchant banking but like the other banks they have found London the most profitable place of business. Most of the overseas banks are generating more profits in London through their activities in the secondary money markets than they are in their entire overseas networks. Their strong contacts in developing countries have given them an advantage in arranging finance for developing indigenous industry and agriculture and finding credit for foreign supplies of capital goods. Here again the merchant banks have sometimes met the challenge by linking up with the overseas banks in establishing subsidiary banks abroad. Mergers have enabled them to enjoy economies of scale and geographically diversify their risks.

The merchant banks' relationship with the clearing banks is changing: in some ways there is more cooperation between them, in other ways, more competition. In the past the activities of the merchant banks have been thought to be complementary to those of the clearing banks, who often introduced business to the merchant banks. The main clients of the merchant banks are not private citizens but business and governments. The clearing banks allowed their smaller neighbours to dominate the business of new issues, investment advice and company take-overs. But all this is changing. The clearing banks have been taking a more active interest through their subsidiaries in developments in the secondary and international money markets.

They have been participating in international lending consortia and establishing link-ups in other financial centres. They have subsidiaries among the finance houses and have begun to acquire interests which have given them a stake in the new issue business. The National Westminster Issue Department has been merged into its subsidiary County Bank, which performs most of the merchant banking functions. These are carried out for Barclays by the Barclays Bank Trust Company, and Midland Bank have, with Samuel Montague, formed a joint company Midland Montague Industrial Finance.

The competition has been too much for some small merchant banks who have either sold their interests to their larger brethren or collapsed as with Knowles and Foster, and Sale & Co. in 1964–65. But there is some disagreement on whether size is essential for survival in merchant banking. Julian Hodge, one of the newer and highly successful merchant bankers, said to George Young 'once a merchant bank gets to the size where it cannot give personal attention to problems at principal level, it will lose some of the advantages normally associated with its somewhat specialized functions'. And John McGregor of Hill Samuel argues that 'to retain virtues of innovation, risk taking and flexibility, a merchant bank depends essentially on the skills of a few highly talented individuals in constant touch with each other'. Many of the merchant banks who have had unfortunate experiences in financial ventures in the past recognize that the trouble arose because their knowledge of the men with whom they dealt was not thorough enough. The need for first hand contacts is one of the reasons behind the opening of branch offices in the provinces. Singer and Friedlander have extensive operations in the North of England. The branch offices are well placed to advise the larger local authorities on the raising of funds. So in as far as the merchant banks are dealers in expert advice the matter of size is of no great importance.

Those who argue that the merchant banks must increase the scale of their operations if they are to meet the competition of the giant American banks and the growing interest of the clearing banks point to three main advantages. Firstly, the larger banks are in a position to offer a much more comprehensive range of services all over the world. Secondly, the larger banks have the huge capital strength which is necessary to support international financial activities, and to meet the danger of international financial crises upsetting the bank. Thirdly, apart from the risk-spreading economies implied in the previous point, the larger banks are able to enjoy other economies arising from the scale of their business, though these must be balanced against the diseconomies which may result from an extension of problems of management. These economies should enable the larger banks to enjoy a better record of profit growth which would increase their comparative advantage and give them a cumulative advantage over their smaller rivals. Of course greater size does not always mean greater profits. This is how the profit league table for the top ten merchant banks looked in 1968–69:

Table 28. MERCHANT BANK PROFITS

Merchant Bank	*Profit* £'000	*Assets* £m	*Acceptances* £m
Warburg	2199	84·1	15·9
Samuel Montague	1809	236·8	11·4
Hill Samuel	1579	216·4	58·9
Hambros	1443	270·4	61·5
Kleinwort Benson	1296	173·0	36·4
Schroder Wagg	894	292·7	40·3
Singer & Friedlander	495	51·7	1·1
Brown Shipley	432	63·1	12·0
Guiness Mahon	431	44·1	8·7
Keyser Ullman	415	41·9	2·5

Rothschild and Antony Gibbs as private companies did not have to declare their profits.

Warburgs whose history dates only from the Second World War have had an enormous impact on the world of the London merchant banks. By stimulating competition between the banks they have helped to bring about the re-emergence of London as the main centre of international finance. John McGregor neatly summarizes the task ahead facing the growing institutions of the merchant banking arena: 'to locate growth areas and functions, actual and potential, and subject to the degree of risk involved maximize the return from the greater weight of assets . . . deployed by them.'

Chapter 8 deals with recent developments in merchant banking.

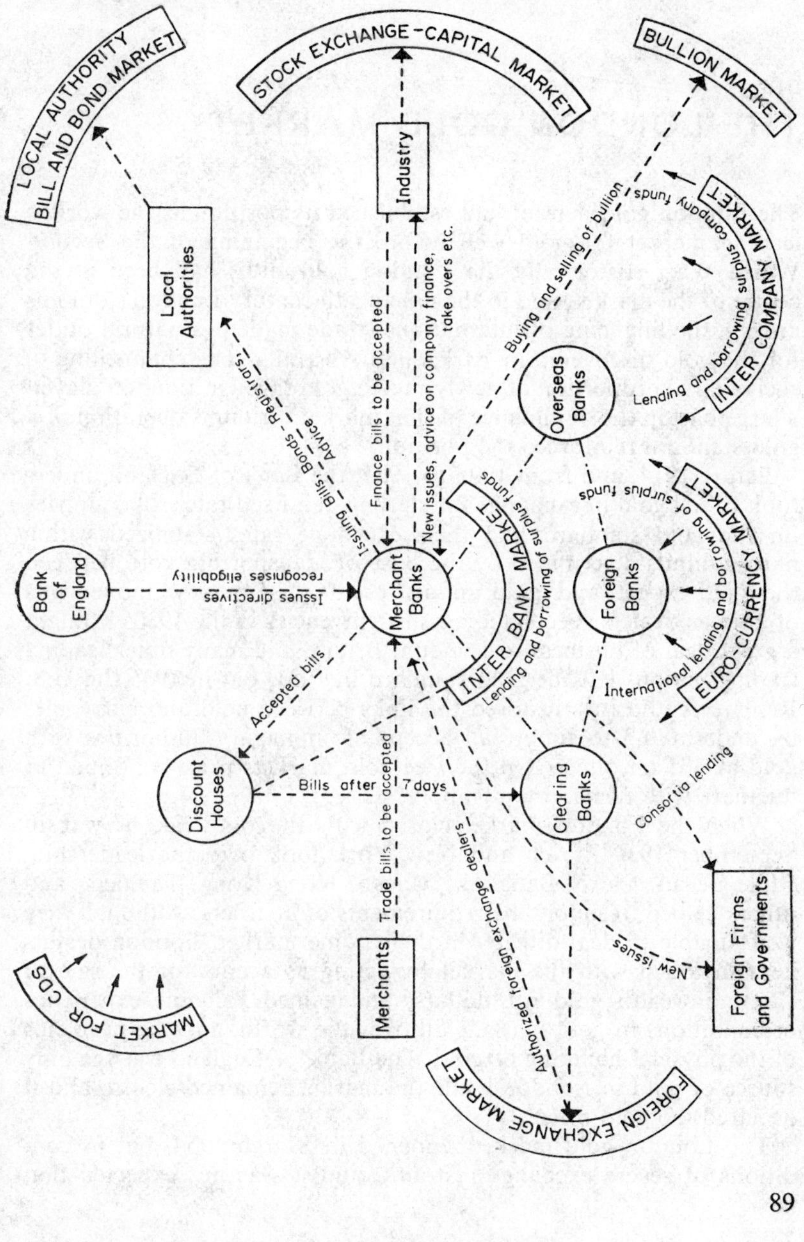
LOCAL AUTHORITY BILL AND BOND MARKET
STOCK EXCHANGE-CAPITAL MARKET
BULLION MARKET
Industry
Local Authorities
INTER COMPANY MARKET
Lending and borrowing surplus company funds
Buying and selling of bullion
New issues, advice on company finance, take overs etc.
Finance bills to be accepted
Issuing Bills, Bonds, Registrars, Advice
Overseas Banks
INTER BANK MARKET
Lending and borrowing of surplus funds
surplus funds
EURO-CURRENCY MARKET
International lending and borrowing of surplus funds
Bank of England
Issues directives
recognises eligibility
Merchant Banks
Foreign Banks
Accepted bills
Discount Houses
Bills after 7 days
Clearing Banks
Consortia lending
Trade bills to be accepted
Authorized foreign exchange dealers
New issues
Foreign Firms and Governments
Merchants
MARKET FOR CDS
FOREIGN EXCHANGE MARKET

5.
THE LONDON GOLD MARKET

The London gold market had established its position as the world's leading market for gold well before the beginning of the Second World War. Historically the London goldsmiths had been at the centre of the market, and in the nineteenth century London's dominance in the financing of international trade made it a natural outlet for the gold discovered in Africa and Australia. The channelling of such a large proportion of newly-mined gold through London played a large part in the dominance of that market. Britain's operation of a gold standard reinforced the position.

Before 1914, and from 1925 to 1931, the Bank of England undertook to sell gold in exchange for sterling at a fixed rate. All countries on the gold standard had their exchange rates stabilized within narrow limits determined by the cost of transporting gold between the 'gold export' and 'gold import' points. The massive movements of gold as dealers speculated against currencies in the 1930s brought a great deal of business to London. Britain and many other leading trading nations left the gold standard in 1931, but in 1935 the U.S. Reserve Authorities restored the links between gold and currencies by undertaking to supply all acceptable monetary authorities with gold at $35 an ounce. On the free gold markets price continued to fluctuate with demand and supply.

When the London market closed with the outbreak of war in September 1939 Zurich and New York took over the leadership, while Beirut, Cairo, Bangkok, Macao, Hong Kong, Tangiers, and others helped to supply the requirements of hoarders. Although they were unable to deal directly in their home market, London dealers kept in touch with the market by acting as agents for the sale of Commonwealth gold for dollars, and gained valuable experience of conditions in gold markets all over the world, and the problems of the physical handling of gold. The Bank of England was the only source of gold in London while the market remained closed, and it declared the gold price.

The London gold market reopened in March 1954, but in conditions of severe exchange restraint, and it was not expected that

London would resume its leading position in the international gold market for some time. However within eighteen months London was handling about four-fifths of the gold coming on to the free markets. This was achieved in spite of the fact that shortage of dollars prevented the Bank of England from allowing Sterling Area residents free access, and only registered sterling could be used. It was chiefly because London dealers dealt on margins deliberately smaller than their rivals, were prepared to handle large quantities quoting very low rates of commission, and maintained a relatively stable price, that they were able to reestablish their dominance even before the pound became fully convertible at the end of 1958. After that date there was a steady increase of business as external sterling and other convertible currencies could be used for gold dealing. There was also an increase in speculative, 'hot-money', gold movements, usually when the U.S. dollar was in difficulties. With the U.S. Federal Reserve guarantee to buy gold offered to it at $35 an ounce, central banks making settlements through the European Payments Union (dissolved in 1958) became strong buyers whenever the price fell below this level.[1] In this way they could settle their debts with a lower real cost. At the same time central banks of countries with a surplus on the balance of payments with the U.S. arranged to collect this surplus in gold, (using their dollar surplus to buy gold on the London market) so that by 1963 U.S. gold reserves were down by $6 billion on the 1953 figure of $22 billion. In an effort to steady the market the central banks began to co-operate, refraining from buying when the price rose above a certain level (or even putting gold on to the market to bring the price down), and bidding up the price by building up reserves when the price was low. The aim was to keep the price within reasonable limits in the event of exceptional and concentrated demand for gold arising from an international political crisis or from speculative movements of funds (*B.E.Q.B.*) The 'gold pool' was formed for this purpose in 1961 by the central banks of Belgium, France, Holland, Italy, Switzerland, W. Germany, U.K., and U.S., with the Bank of England acting as agent for their dealings. The pool had a good deal of success in the early 1960s in damping down speculation, but with the reduction in central bank dealings the total turnover of the market was greatly reduced.

The workings of the London gold market

Although the Exchange Control Act of 1947 allows all authorized

[1] This guaranteed price ended in 1971.

banks to deal in gold, there are only five practising members of the London gold market. Two are merchant banks: Samuel Montagu and N. M. Rothschild. Two are brokers and owned by two other merchant banks: Mocatta and Goldsmid owned by Hambros, and Sharps, Pixley owned by Kleinwort, Benson. The other firm is Johnson, Matthey which is very closely linked to a metallurgical firm of international repute. This firm shares the melting, refining, assaying and processing operations with Rothschilds. Montagu and Mocatta and Goldsmid are the most powerful dealers in the market, but traditionally Rothschild have acted as chairmen and provided the premises for the meeting each working day at 10.30 a.m. when the five firms meet to determine the official London gold price: this is the 'gold-fixing'. A tentative price is mooted and brokers are asked to declare amounts that would be bought or sold at that price. If the amount offered exceeds the amount required at that price a lower price will be fixed, but the market is always slightly biased in favour of endeavouring to absorb all new production or other gold which may be offered at the fixing. The London market will handle only 'good delivery bars', melted and stamped by one of the approved refiners and carrying a respectable assay of at least 995 parts of pure gold in 1,000: these standards are now the basis for international acceptability. Rothschild also act as agents for the Bank of England, who in turn operate the Exchange Equalization Account. Until recently the Bank also acted for the gold pool, and placed gold on behalf of the Reserve Bank of South Africa. It is thus hardly a surprise that the sales and purchases in the market were dominated by the Bank, which, even though it is not present at the fixing, exercises the real power through their Rothschild spokesman.

In practice however anything between 10 and 90 per cent of the business of the London gold market is done outside the fixing, and gold prices may fluctuate a great deal during the day. This business is, like that of the foreign exchange market, done by phone, and London dealers have links with all parts of the world. Unlike the foreign exchange market though, there is no organized or regular market in gold for forward delivery, but forward supply of large amounts of gold are in practice often negotiated.

In the absence of official support and intervention the gold price is determined by demand and supply. Demand for gold arises in four principal ways. First, with gold providing the main backing for the world's money supply – the chief media for the settlement of international debts arising from trade and payments – it is in demand by central banks for official reserves. Such authorities sometimes need gold to sell to obtain foreign currencies, or to support their own currency in the foreign exchange market. Quotas to the International Monetary Fund are paid partly in gold and partly in the members' own currency. A few official coins have been struck in recent years and a small amount of gold is needed for this purpose.

Second, and most important of the non-official buyers, are those who demand gold for hoarding. They are a diverse breed, but divide principally between those who want gold as a long term protection against inflation, or devaluation, and speculators who buy gold in times of failing confidence in currencies in the hope of short term gains. Speculators make gains only when the difference between the lower price at which they buy gold and the higher price at which they sell is sufficient to enable them to enjoy a margin after paying the shipping, handling and insurance charges, the brokers commission, and perhaps a small premium. Simple arbitrage operations prevent the gold price falling below the 'shipping parity' i.e. where gold can be bought in one market and sold with profit in another. There is a third category centred in the East where gold is bought as a symbol of status and wealth. Despite the efforts of the Indian Government some £70 million of gold is thought to be smuggled into India every year, and the accumulated hoardings probably exceed £1,500 million. Within Europe the greatest demand for gold for hoarding comes from French citizens, although the business is not uncommon in Germany and Switzerland. Swiss bankers have been criticized for their part in encouraging speculative gold and currency movements. In some exceptional years hoarders have taken a larger part of gold supplies than official buyers, even though the costs in taking delivery and holding this gold are far from small. It has been said that the cost of burying and keeping gold in the vaults of Fort Knox (U.S.A.) are as great as the cost of digging it out of the ground in South Africa.

The amount of gold going to remaining purchasers is small compared with the foregoing, but industry, dentists, and more especially jewellers are of some importance.

The supply of gold consists of newly mined gold coming on to the market and transfers from existing stocks. These transfers occur when central banks need to buy foreign currencies, when speculators decide to collect their gains in currency following a rise in the price of gold (or a fall in the price of the currency), and when hoarders need to sell gold to make purchases of goods. In most years the supplies of newly mined gold come largely from South Africa (more than 80 per cent of non-Russian gold), earning some £500 million a year for that country. Russian supplies have been irregular but have sometimes reached as much as £200 million in a year (1963). Until recently this newly mined gold has been sold at the London market at the price fixed there.

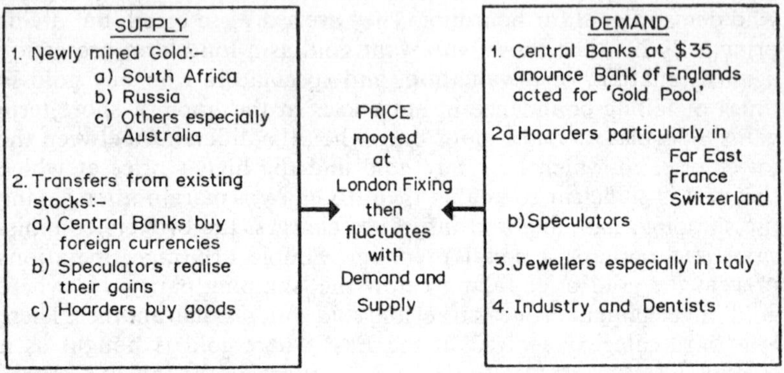

Recent developments in the London gold market

The 1960s was a time of such heavy speculation both in gold and in foreign currencies (particularly dollars, sterling, francs and marks), that the very system of international money seemed to be threatened. Various remedies were suggested such as the Reuff Plan to raise the price of gold (France had accumulated sizeable gold reserves, and had withdrawn from the gold pool in 1967), the U.S. idea that free gold markets should be closed, and finally that a 'two-tier' gold market should be adopted. Doubts about the ability of the central banks to maintain supplies even with the existence of the gold pool caused speculators to rush into the market, and turnover soared. The dealers themselves were able to take a position. The comfortable regular business had become frantic but also more profitable. The three banks, Union Bank of Switzerland, Swiss Bank Corporation, and Swiss Credit Bank which make up the Zurich market, made the most of their position to meet the requirements of French gold hoarders, Italian jewellers, and international gold smugglers. Hong Kong attracted the bulk of Australian supplies to meet Far Eastern requirements. But turnover in London was yet to be threatened with these markets operating more as appendages to the London market.

However on March 15 1968 the London gold market closed and the seven central banks still cooperating in the gold pool decided to end the arrangements by which they would sell to any monetary authority to replace gold sold by those authorities on the free market at the official price of $35 an ounce. They called on other central banks to support this policy. In this way the gold pool was terminated and the two-tier price established, as the monetary authorities continued to deal between themselves at the existing official price, while the free market was allowed to find its own price level without official support or intervention. Arrangements whereby South Africa had supplied monetary authorities through the London market at the official price also broke down, with South Africa holding out for a higher price.

The termination of the gold pool and the cessation of supplies from South Africa called for drastic changes in the function of the London gold market when it reopened on April 1 1968. The market was quick to take measures for adaptation to the new conditions. A second daily fixing began at 3.0 p.m. each day, so that the London fixing price, which is accepted all over the world as the best indicator of conditions on the gold market, can be brought more closely in step when prices fluctuate widely in active markets. The second fixing also provides dealers in North America with a guideline at a more convenient time for their market. Secondly, it was decided that prices should be quoted in U.S. dollars. The London market had clung to its quotation in sterling when it reopened in 1954 even though dollars had become internationally more widely used. Thirdly, every effort was made to keep commissions to be paid by buyers down to small margins so that London continued to offer a cheaper market than elsewhere. Generations of experience enable London brokers to handle gold more cheaply than their competitors, while their unrivalled connections with dealers all over the world have brought rival brokers to London to offset transactions that cannot be matched in their own markets. Paul Jeanty of Samuel Montagu expressed his confidence that London 'can remain successful as the only truly international gold market'.

The experience of 1969 has not fundamentally shaken this conclusion but has shown the need for more cautious optimism. South Africa has continued to withhold supplies from the London market and brokers have had to rely on sales by hoarders and speculators. So on two counts the Zurich market has had an advantage over London. In the first place they were offered and bought a substantial quantity of gold from South Africa, and secondly, they have handled the huge hoards of gold which found their way to Switzerland during the great speculation. It is estimated that the result of these advantages was that Zurich handled half as much gold again as London during 1969.

The dealers and speculators who expected the 'freeing' of the gold market to bring booming business and profits were not quickly satisfied. In the short run after reaching a peak of almost $44 an ounce the free gold price descended steadily to less than $38. However the two-tier system was not phased out when the free price fell below the official price. At this stage there was no resumption of speculative buying although Industrial buyers stocked up heavily. The market was waiting for new agreements between South Africa and the international monetary authorities, for the possible working scheme of special drawing rights at the International Monetary Fund to supplement gold in the financing of international trade, or for a rise in the official gold price. The amount of gold coming on to the market was just sufficient to meet the traditional demands of Eastern hoarders and industrial requirements. Moreover there was increasing reluctance to bear the financial risks involved with the price depressed by the lack of buyers and a huge 'speculative overhang', calculated at 7,500 metric tons – the amount of gold in private hands – which might be sold at any time in the free market.

There were at that time four main factors responsible for the swing away from the peak gold price of almost $44 an ounce, to the official gold price, and even slightly below. Firstly, the deterioration of the South African balance of payments in 1970 which forced that country to put more gold on to the market. Secondly, the effective launching of S.D.R.'s in larger quantities and much earlier than had been expected, which inevitably reduced the demand for monetary gold below what would otherwise have been the case. At the September 1971 meeting of the I.M.F. the Chancellor of the Exchequer put Britain's full support behind the widespread use of S.D.R.'s in place of sterling and dollars as the international currency. Thirdly, the various readjustments in international monetary media – the devaluation of sterling and the franc and the revaluation of the mark – and the surplus on the U.K. balance of payments, reduced instability and made settlements much easier. Fourthly, rising interest rates in European money markets have provided speculators with an attractive alternative to dealing in gold, particularly as the cost of financing speculative gold purchases has been increasing. Had it not been for

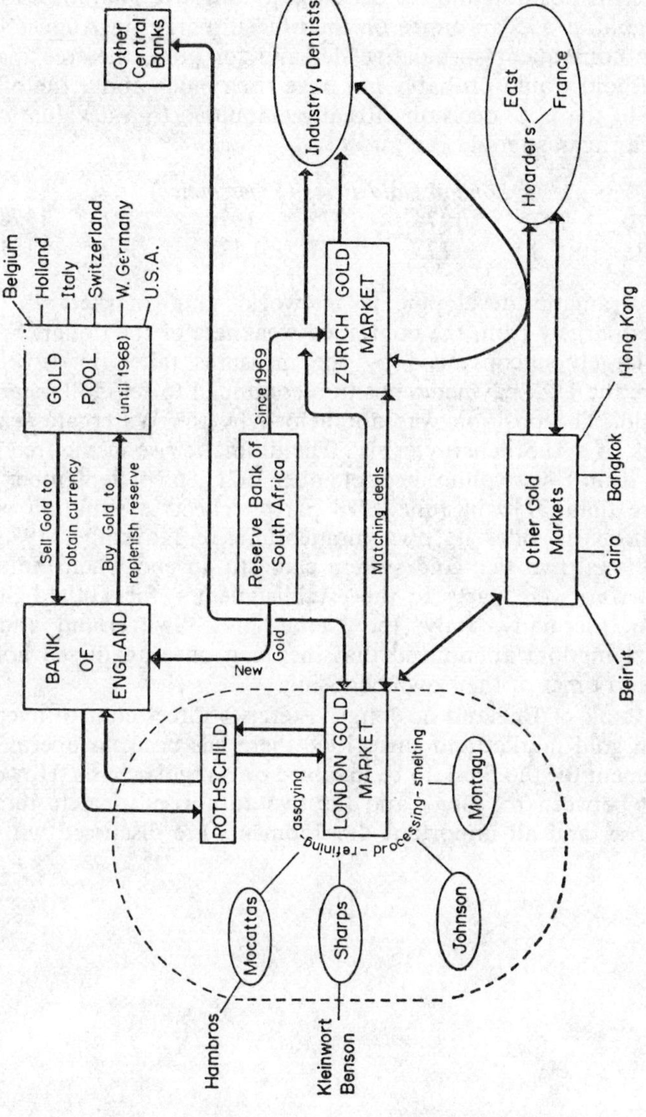

THE LONDON GOLD MARKET

the measures taken by the U.S. authorities to correct the U.S. balance of payments position and the decision no longer to guarantee to buy or sell gold at $35 an ounce on the official market in August 1971, and the consequent speculative demand for gold, the free market price of gold would probably not have risen much above the official price. But the U.S. decision virtually amounted to a devaluation of the dollar against gold.

London Gold Price ($ *per ounce*)

1970	1973	1974	1975	1976	1977	1978
35	90	173	177	128	149	181

The dramatic developments in world gold markets in 1973 stemmed largely from the continued weakness of the dollar. Speculators largely unconvinced by the measures taken in 1972/3 to improve the U.S. payments position continued to sell dollars and to buy gold. The position was not helped by the Watergate scandal and talk of a U.S. 'energy crisis'. The dramatic rise in the free price of gold from $40 an ounce in September 1971, $65 in September 1972 to more than $110 in June 1973 partly reflects a situation where speculation provides its own momentum. In November 1973 the international two tier gold system came to an end when the seven nations who were party to the establishment – the United States, Belgium, Germany, Italy, the Netherlands, Switzerland and the United Kingdom announced that they can once again sell gold at prices and times of their own choosing.

The Bank of England no longer exercises direct control over the London gold market and since 1968 there has been no operational requirement for the Bank to be involved on a regular basis. However, contact between the Bank and the five authorised dealers remains very close, and all important developments are discussed with the Bank.

6.
SECONDARY MONEY MARKETS

In the previous chapters we have been primarily concerned with the behaviour of the traditional financial institutions in the traditional money markets. But the predominant theme has been one of change and adaptation, and this has brought frequent references to the development of new markets for money, and we now turn to an examination of these markets and of the institutions which participate in them. There are four of these 'new' money markets:

1. The Euro-currency market
2. The Inter-bank market
3. The market for short term local authority finance
4. The market for short term funds for finance houses.

There are many points of contact between these markets and with the traditional money markets. There has been some debate about the correct nomenclature for the markets. It has been argued that the markets are no longer new, that the term 'secondary' is better applied to the dealings in Certificates of Deposit, that the term parallel does not bring out the proper relationships of these markets to one another and to the traditional money markets, and that the most suitable term would be 'the complementary money markets'. However there is a wide acceptance of the term 'secondary money markets', used to distinguish them from the primary activities of the discount market and to cover the activities in the four markets mentioned above, and we will use it for this chapter.

The main banks participating in these markets, as we have seen in previous chapters, are the merchant banks, the British overseas and Commonwealth banks, the foreign banks and their affiliates, of which the American banks, because of their importance, may be taken as a separate group, the other overseas banks, and the other banks, many of which are subsidiaries of the London clearing banks. The clearing banks do not participate directly in the markets.[1] None of these institutions has been specially established to deal in the secondary

---

[1] Because by convention they have to keep large reserves in the Bank of England, and are not free to use them in this secondary business.

markets, rather the activities of these markets have been tacked on to their traditional business. However special offices and branches have been set up, particularly by American and foreign banks operating in London, to take full advantage of the developing business.

There is a further wide range of financial institutions which use the markets as a means of making their temporary surplus funds earn interest and they include central banks and certain international monetary institutions, insurance companies, discount houses and finance houses, savings banks and investment trusts. The funds of the non-bank institutions form a significant part of some of these markets, and even smaller traders and private individuals have been known to participate. Their surplus funds often pass through the hands of specialist brokers, some of their off-shoots of the discount houses, who have set up to meet the specialist needs of the markets. This money will often be lent at call and so constitutes a valuable income earning, and yet liquid, asset for these institutions. It is often deposits that are being moved around in these transactions, and because they are unsecured 'each institution commonly observes limits regarding the extent to which it will place deposits with other individual institutions in the market'. (*MBR* 1966). The markets do not deal only in very short term surplus funds for which a high degree of liquidity is required, they take deposits for periods up to three years, to suit the needs of the depositor and to match lending commitments.[1] Where, in the past, large industrial and commercial concerns had little other than the deposit accounts of commercial banks in which to place their short term surplus funds, they can now use a highly developed, sophisticated market network.

The origins of the markets lie back in the 1960s but the period of most dramatic growth occurred in the last five years. The growth of the markets is closely associated with the expansion of sterling and foreign currency deposits with the various banks participating in the market. The following statistics give us the best indicator of the growth of business:

---

[1] These are therefore essentially time deposit markets and the banks participating endeavour to match the maturity of their claims and liabilities. More than half of their total liabilities are for maturities of two days to three months, another quarter are for three months to one year, less than a twentieth are for over one year, and liabilities at call are about a sixth of the total.

Table 29. THE DEPOSITS OF BANKS IN THE SECONDARY MARKETS 1966–1970

	Deposits (£m)		*Other Currency deposits* (£m)		*Total deposits* (£m)	
	June 66	Dec 70	June 66	Dec 70	June 66	Dec 70
Accepting Houses	716	1392	382	1614	1098	3006
Br. Overseas & C'wealth	1083	1656	766	4143	1849	5799
American	423	963	1457	10604	1879	11567
Foreign banks & affiliates	261	393	218	1739	479	2132
Other Overseas Banks	212	183	372	1263	584	1446
Other banks	235	1869	99	1709	334	3578
Total	2930	6456	3295	21072	6225	27528

Sources: *MBR & BEQB*

The business of the markets denominated in sterling has more than doubled since 1966, while the foreign currency business has increased almost seven fold. Much of this latter dramatic increase in business has been in the Euro-currency market and through the activities of the American banks, whose deposits account for half of the total of other currency deposits. The business of the various banks with offices in London in:

1. the Euro-currency market amounts to more than £20,000 million
2. the Inter-bank market amounts to more than £1,700 million
3. the Local Authority market amounts to more than £2,700 million
4. the finance houses market amounts to approx. £600 million

The tenfold increase in the deposits of other banks is some indication of the awareness of the clearing banks that they must compete for deposits. They do this through their subsidiaries and affiliates among the small merchant banks. The change from the 1963 position when

American, British overseas and Commonwealth banks shared equally about two-thirds of the markets denominated in other currencies, and the accepting houses took a fifth, to the American dominance (more than 50 per cent) leaving the accepting houses less than 8 per cent of the market-total has been the most striking feature of the development of the market. The number of American branches has increased from nine to more than thirty.

Factors contributing to the growth of the secondary markets

1. The change in the government's monetary policy in the 1950s away from cheap money to the manipulation of interest rates made possible a return of competition among the institutions of the money market. In the traditional markets and among the clearing banks and their customers the rigid pattern of interest rates remained and it was left to the merchant banks and other financial institutions to establish competitive interest rates and to exploit the flexibility of the new markets.

2. The participants in the new markets were prepared to accept a very small margin between borrowing and lending rates, much narrower than the margins applying in domestic banking. This was because the banks in the secondary markets were not required to keep large reserves, which earn little or nothing, and because they deal in very large amounts usually around a £million and seldom, if ever, less than £100,000. These are wholesale markets for 'short' term money. Deposits change hands frequently and the economies which result from the bulk sums help to make the narrow margins profitable. The margins have to be sufficient to meet the cost of forward cover where foreign exchange is involved or the profit might be wiped out by an unfavourable movement of exchange values.

3. The removal of official restrictions on the flow of short term funds made possible international movements when longer term international investment was still under control. The secondary markets are much less subject to controls than the traditional markets; there are fewer regulations and no limits on the rates payable for deposits.[1]

---

[1] Unlike loans in the discount market those in the secondary markets are unsecured although loans to local authorities are guaranteed by their trustees status and secured against the local rates. It is the responsibility of the vendor to be well informed on the ability of the borrower to repay at maturity.

The credit restrictions which hamper activities in the primary markets have given the secondary markets a further boost.

4. Exchange control has limited participating in the Euro-currency market by U.K. residents and there has been some restriction on the use of Euro-currencies in the U.K. Banks and foreign exchange dealers authorized by the Bank of England are participants in the market. The removal of restrictions on the convertibility of sterling for external holders in December 1958 helped to foster the development of the market.

5. The rapid rise in interest rates after 1957 encouraged competition in the markets, and funds flowed freely between the sterling markets if interest rate differentials arose. Moreover Euro dollars were converted in sterling to take advantage of favourable rates in other markets. When Euro dollar rates were more favourable funds flowed the other way. There is no typical structure of rates in the secondary markets, unlike the traditional markets where rates are closely related to Bank rate. Secondary market rates are largely determined by the rates obtainable day by day in the other money markets and for gilt edged bonds, and certificates of deposit, related, of course, to various other market conditions. These rates are usually quoted and fixed regardless of how Bank rate might change, although a given change might affect new quotations. A tightening of money in the primary market is likely to divert borrowers to the secondary market and to drive up rates there. This is a particularly powerful factor in the Inter bank market and as a result rates fluctuate more widely and rapidly sometimes reaching as high as 20 per cent and at other times as low as 1 per cent. The following table shows the rates which applied at the end of the year from 1964 to 1970:

Table 30. COMPARATIVE INTEREST RATES IN PRIMARY AND SECONDARY MARKETS

% End of	1964	1967	1970	1975	*Aug.* 1978
Bank Rate MLR	7	8	7	11·25	10
Treasury Bill	6·74	7·62	6·87	10·64	9·05
Prime Bank Bill	6·84	7·78	8·0	10·83	9·31
Clearing Bank Deposit Account	5	6	5	9	8
Clearing Bank Call Money	5·375	6·25	5·375	11·25	9·25
Inter Bank overnight		8·0	6·00	11·75	8·75
Local Authority 3 month	8·0	8·44	7·19	11·31	9·25
Finance House 3 month	7·69	8·19	7·75	11·06	9·37*
Euro dollar 3 month	4·50	6·31	6·56	5·87	9

* Sterling Certificates of Deposit
Sources: *MBR & BEQB*

6. Users of the markets including business and private individuals have become highly conscious of differentials in rates, and anxious to secure the most profitable outlet for their funds. The size of the surpluses to be employed have grown as mergers and groupings have taken place.

7. The specialists in the secondary markets have become skilled jobbers of these short term funds and have reduced to a very small margin the rate between borrowing and relending. There is a great deal of on-lending in the markets, funds changing hands many times before reaching the eventual user.

8. There have been special factors and characteristics in the development of each of the secondary markets and we turn next to examine these.

The Euro-currency market

The business of on-lending foreign currency deposits was first practised in the 1930s but it was not until the late 1950s that conditions became favourable for a considerable development of this practice. In 1957 the market for Euro-currencies amounted to less than £100 million, while in 1971 it exceeded £14,000 million. These Euro-currencies have been defined in *B.E.Q.B.* as 'those other than the domestic currency of the country in which the bank taking the deposit or lending the funds is located'. The Euro dollar is by far the most important of the currencies (90 per cent), although there is some dealing in Euro Deutche marks (5 per cent) and Euro-Swiss francs (3 per cent). The Euro dollar writes Sayers 'is an ordinary dollar balance in the books of a bank in the U.S.A., what is extraordinary is that it is lent out, as a dollar balance, by the depositor (this depositor being not a resident of the U.S.A.) and that the borrower of the dollars comes to this market in London although the obvious place to borrow dollars is New York.' The total of Euro dollars is now half as large as the total official international liquidity in gold and foreign currency reserves at the I.M.F.

The market for Euro dollars (see diagram) grew up because there were dollar holdings in countries in Europe and elsewhere that were not being put to the most profitable use. Iron curtain countries had placed their holdings of dollars with London banks after the war and these were relent to borrowers who needed dollars. Other dollar balances have arisen from trade and other transactions. The U.S.A. has had a persistent deficit on the balance of payments. These balances were on-lent by banks in Europe often passing through several hands, each making a small margin on the transaction before reaching the eventual user. This on-lending of balances was possible only after exchange controls had been lifted in Europe. While domestic interest rates in Europe were low there was not much profit in the business but the rapidly rising trend of interest rates in the 1950s and in the 1960s opened up possibilities for profitable business. Western European countries have usually provided over half the total funds of the market.

The market developed in Europe not only because it was here that dollar holdings were available but also because of monetary regulations in the United States. Most famous of these is Regulation Q; as part of a policy of credit restriction it aimed primarily at commercial bank loans to business, and imposed strict ceilings on rates that could be paid by the banks for time deposits. This created a gap between market rates for these deposits and the ceiling rates so that the banks were losing time deposits, and all this in the face of a constant clamour from business for further credit.[1] It was these precourses which forced the U.S. banks to look to the Euro-market for their dollars, and led to the establishment of many more branches in Europe to relay Euro dollars to the head offices.

London emerged as the main centre of the market, and there were a number of reasons for this. We have seen already that London's financial institutions had a great deal of exportive and experience in international monetary business and in the business of handling various kinds of short term money. They were reasonably alive to the opportunities of developing new forms of business, and as a result they were first in the field when the market began to develop. The Suez crisis in 1957 forced London bankers to look for means of overcoming the restrictions placed on the use of sterling credits to finance non-British trade. They began to use the dollar holdings of residents outside the U.S.A. for this purpose. The market developed outside the control of national monetary authorities, and successful participants were those who were able to offer the most competitive rates. The skill of the London bankers was evident here again and this ability to quote rates which were finer than in any other centres reinforced London's position. This achievement must be seen against a background of strict U.K. exchange control which prevented most U.K. residents from participating in the market. Remarkably U.S. residents were able to borrow more cheaply in London than in New York while dollar holders were able to get better rates for lending in London than elsewhere. The activities of the London banks in the Euro-currency market provides valuable invisible earnings for Britain.

Between 1963 and 1969 the number of banks and other institutions participating in the London Euro-currency market increased from 132 to 193: In 1971 the number rose to more than 200. The size of funds in the market rose in that period from £1,300 million to £12,500

---

[1] For example in 1969 the U.S. Federal Reserve Board imposed a ceiling of 6¼ per cent on time deposits and bank funds flowed into Certificates of Deposits where a higher rate could be earned.

million, and in 1971 exceeded £20,000 million. Taking the Euro dollar market as a whole (not just in London) the Bank for International Settlements has estimated an increase in the net volume of funds from $9 billion in 1964 to $37·56 billion in 1969. By the end of 1971 it will no doubt be in excess of $50 billion. The problem of making exact measurements is that many of the transactions of the market are merely on-lending, and the anonymity of the market increases the difficulty of discovering the original lender and the eventual user. The possibilities of double-counting are considerable.

Dr F. E. Aschinger, the Economic Adviser to the Swiss Banking Corporation has produced some interesting figures (in *BM* February 1971) to show the sources and users of Euro dollars in the Euro market as a whole (i.e. E.E.C., U.K., Switzerland and Sweden).

Table 31. SOURCES AND USERS OF EURO DOLLARS 1964–1969 $ BILLION

Sources	*1964*	*1966*	*1968*	*1969*
Inside Euro market	4·4	8·4	13·5	18·6
Outside Euro market	4·6	6·1	11·8	18·9
– From N. America	1·5	1·7	4·5	6·7
– Rest of W. Europe	–	1·1	1·9	2·7
Total	9·0	14·5	25·0	37·5
Users				
Inside Euro market	5·0	6·3	7·9	11·7
Outside Euro market	4·0	8·2	17·1	25·8
– of which N. America	2·2	5·0	10·4	17·8
Total	9·0	14·5	25·0	37·5
Net position				
Inside Euro market	+ 0·6	− 2·1	− 5·3	− 6·9
Outside Euro market	− 0·6	+ 2·1	+ 5·3	+ 6·9
of which N. America	+ 0·7	+ 3·3	+ 5·9	+ 11·1
Japan	+ 0·4	+ 0·6	+ 1·6	+ 1·1

\+ indicates area is a net supplier

− indicates area is a net user

Sources: *Bank of International Settlements* and *Bankers' Magazine*

A more recent analysis of the activities of institutions in London in the Euro-currency market was given in December 1970 in *BEQB*.

Table 32. ACTIVITIES IN LONDON EURO-CURRENCY MARKET

	Liabilities		*Claims*	
	July 1969	July 1970	July 1969	July 1970
British banks (incl. Comm.)	4914	6891	4963	6926
American Banks	8891	9746	8870	9696
Other foreign banks	2051	2769	2054	2754
Total (£m)	15856	19406	15887	19376

Source: *BEQB*

The tables show quite clearly that the sources of Euro dollars are divided evenly between Western European countries, i.e. E.E.C., U.K., Switzerland and Sweden, and other countries. The United States and Canada provide about a sixth of the total deposits and sterling area countries about a twelfth. If exchange permission is forthcoming U.K. residents can deposit funds in the market, and in 1969 about £500 million was deposited. There are four main ways in which U.K. residents participate in the market. About a third is the temporary employment of foreign currencies which had been borrowed for an approved purpose and is employed in the Euro market prior to re-investment. About a half constitutes the holdings of trading and commercial companies with such international business as oil companies, insurance firms and shipping lines. They need international funds to finance their business. The remainder divides between the proceeds of the disinvestment of foreign currency securities by U.K. residents which is awaiting re-investment, and the money which has been borrowed by U.K. institutions to finance the purchase of foreign currency securities and is held in the form of Euro dollars until the market is favourable.

The banks participating in the market have, as we have seen, an eye for a profitable margin whenever interest rate differentials arise and this is the prime reason for the supply of funds for the market from this source. It is moreover a most convenient way of employing liquid funds. The banks make constant comparisons of rates and decide whether to convert into sterling or other currencies to take advantage of more favourable opportunities. The use of Euro dollars

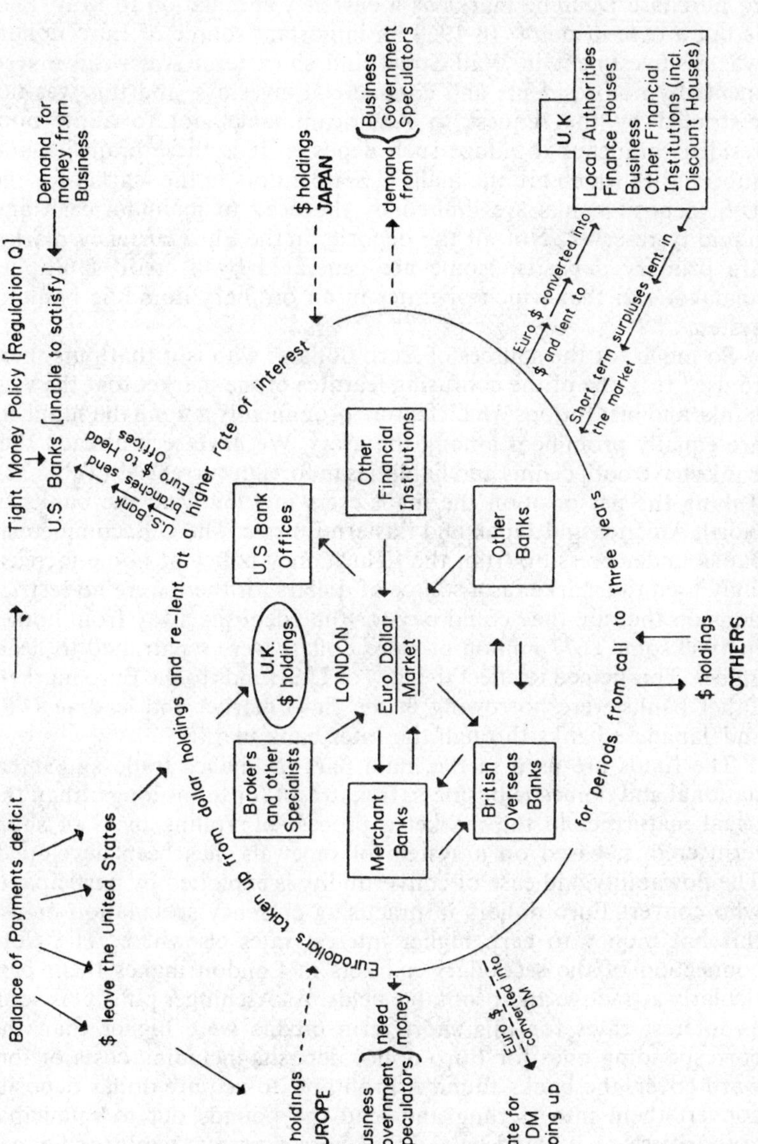

EURO DOLLAR MARKET

to purchase Deutche marks as a currency speculation in May 1971 is but a case in point. In 1969 an important source of Euro dollars was disinvestment in Wall Street and short term American investments by non-residents and commercial investors, and this was not restricted by the request to American banks not to allow non-resident branches to adopt such deposits. It is these branches and subsidiaries which are the main U.S. operators in the market for the U.S. deposit banks are limited by the need to maintain cash and liquidity reserves. Not all the deposits in the Euro-currency market are primary deposits, 'some are generated by a credit multiplier analagous to that which operates in an ordinary domestic banking system'.

So much for the sources of Euro dollars: who is it that puts them to use? It is one of the confusing features of the market that the very banks and institutions which feature prominently among the suppliers are equally prominent among the users. We have seen already that banks have both claims and liabilities in foreign currencies (Table 32). Taking the net position the main users in 1969 were the banks of North America and Japan and Eastern Europe. The U.S. commercial banks under pressure from the tight money policy at home increasingly used the market as a source of dollars for there were no restrictions on the rate they could pay for time deposits away from home. In 1969 some £677 million of Euro dollars were repatriated to head offices. This helped to effect the flow of U.S. funds to the Euro market. Other banks were borrowing in the Euro market and leading U.S. and Japanese banks through the Inter-bank market.

The funds are used in the main part to finance trade and international and domestic business. Investment for terms longer than the usual maturities in the market a process of 'rolling over' of short term credits, based on a system of renewals, has been developed. The flowability and ease of convertibility is exploited by participants who convert Euro dollars in practising currency speculation or use this hot money to earn higher interest rates elsewhere. The close connection of the secondary markets in London makes them particularly attractive and profitable fields. As Aschinger puts it 'as soon as interest rates for this short term credits were higher than the corresponding ones for Euro dollar deposits including costs of forward cover, the banks found it profitable to acquire dollar deposits convert them into sterling and lend the pounds out to municipal authorities', or it could be to other borrowers e.g. banks or finance houses.

Various attempts have been made by domestic monetary authorities to control residents' activities in the Euro-currency market if only to prevent these activities from frustrating their policies. In January 1971 U.K. Treasury clamped down on Euro-currency borrowing by U.K. companies in a move to curb flows of short term funds into Britain. 'Since mid October 1960 individual banks in the U.S.A. have been required to hold reserves of 10 per cent against their borrowing from their overseas branches in excess of the average amount outstanding during the four weeks to May 29 1969; if the amount of a bank's borrowing falls below the May level its reserve free base is correspondingly reduced.' (*B.E.Q.B.* note). The German and the Italian authorities have used the market to reduce overliquidity and to ease inflationary pressure from funds coming in from abroad. It is also used as a means of modifying a balance of payment surplus. Other restrictions imposed to prevent the use of the market against the national credit policy have included measures designed to obstruct these encumventing credit restrictions, foreign exchange control on banks restricting placing funds on the market, and a requirement to re-export Euro deposits. Even though Aschinger believes that no country can be fully insulated from the effects of international interest rate developments he argues that 'the Euro market represents a healthy and effective competitive force in the international financial system and should not be the object of general control and opposition on the part of national monetary authorities.' But there is little multi-lateral supervision of the market apart from the interest taken by the Bank for International Settlements, and so it is not surprising that domestic monetary authorities who see their interest rates affected, large capital flows endangered, domestic liquidity altered as a result of actions in the Euro market can be forgiven for reacting strongly to this reduction of the autonomy of their credit policy.

The most important single factor influencing flows of Euro dollars and interest rates in the market is the credit policy of the monetary authorities in the United States. When credit is tight deposits flow from the States to earn higher interest in the Euro market. Euro dollars are then re-channelled by the branches back to the head offices to help to alleviate the credit shortage. When credit is easier the U.S. banks are able to borrow at home and there is less demand from them for Euro dollars. Thus in 1969 a heavy demand from U.S. banks for Euro dollars drove up interest rates to an unprecedented 12 per cent and $ millions were repatriated. In 1970 repayments by

U.S. banks and some easing of U.S. credit restrictions accentuated the usual seasonal decline of Euro market rates which fell to around 7 per cent in November 1971. Interest rates in the market are influenced to a lesser extent by credit policies in Western European countries. Euro-currency developments have been a major-factor in the movement towards the integration of foreign exchange and domestic monetary operations.

Other secondary markets

The participants in these markets and the factors in the development of their activities were discussed earlier in the chapter and it now remains to bring out their special characteristics. The Inter-bank market has most in common with the Euro-currency market. There is a great deal of on-lending of deposits before they reach the eventual user. The interaction of interest rates and flows of funds between these two markets is very close, and, of course, they are both markets in wholesale money. The participating banks are largely the same, with the same object of employing available funds at the highest rate of interest available in the markets.

These funds are unsecured and have no obvious outlet. There are 150 or so of these banks in the Inter-bank market and they employ funds which are temporarily surplus to the requirements of the banks and other financial institutions and other large commercial and industrial concerns who hold them. For these institutions it is an admirable way of putting their funds to profitable employment without losing control over their availability for other use when the time comes. Much of this money is therefore at call though there are significant amounts in the market for three months or more. The institutions supplying funds to the market are therefore using it to adjust their cash and liquidity positions. This fact and the sensitivity of the market to interest changes elsewhere make interest rates in this market highly volatile.

The discount market has suffered from the development of the Inter-bank market for funds which may at one time have found their way into the discount market are now attracted to the Inter-bank market by the higher rate of interest and because of its convenience and lack of restrictions. The clearing banks have also lost to this market some of the deposits that were traditionally left with them. The banks have been known to make some use of this market to ease their liquidity problems but for the most part they continue to rely on the traditional discount market.

Local authorities obtain their finance from several sources. They continue to raise funds in the new capital issues market, and make issues of negotiable bonds, when this is agreed by the Bank of England. There are specialists who negotiate the placement of local authority mortgages and bonds, and there is the Public Works Loans Board, which at one time virtually controlled local authority borrowing but now acts as little more than 'a lender of last resort'. It was the change in the regulations governing local authority borrowing which allowed this market in short term loans to develop after 1956. This market has grown rapidly and will probably be handling up to £3,000 million in 1971. Short term borrowing should not constitute more than 20 per cent of the total outstanding loan debt of an authority.

The market differs from the Inter-bank and Euro-currency markets not in the lenders of money and the specialists handling the transactions, for the same banks, brokers and financial and common institutions are involved, but in the users of the funds. Unlike the other two there is but one ultimate user and that is the local authority putting the money to use in its own area. A further difference is that the local authorities have the advantage of trustee status in their borrowing, which is secured on the local rates. Local authority treasurers have gained a great deal of expertise and experience in dealings in the market, but they usually rely on specialist brokers who are responsible for placement of sums which are not usually less than £50,000 and often more than £½ million. The money is sometimes placed at call and otherwise on terms up to 364 days. The authorities pay interest gross (without tax) on deposits of less than one year.

Although dealings in the market are solely in sterling the close connections with the Euro-currency markets has resulted, at various times when the sales in the local authority market were favourable, in Euro dollars being converted into sterling to be placed in the local authority market, or in the market for finance house short term funds. This market for deposits with finance houses is the smallest of the four with total funds employed of about £1,700 million. The pattern of interest rates in the market are open to many of the influences which affect the other markets but there are further complicities because the financial standing of each individual house has to be considered by the lender when the rate is fixed. The less the standing the greater the risk and the higher the rate of interest will be. The houses often make use of the mechanism and techniques of the bill market. Bills are drawn under acceptance credits usually with merchant banks who discount them and these are sometimes passed on to the discount market. There are more than £100 million of these bills outstanding. If the houses find themselves temporarily in surplus they will make use of other markets to on-lend this money. Until the recent relaxation of controls the market had been severely restricted both by the 98 per cent ceiling on lending and the light terms for hire purchase consumer goods.

The development of secondary markets for short term money has had a profound effect on the traditional banks and markets of the City of London. A new spirit of competition has forced institutions to adopt a more businesslike attitude to old business and to seek ways of competing successfully in the new lines. This has resulted in the setting up of new operators, some of whom are the subsidiaries or affiliates of the clearing banks. In this way they have their stake in the new business. Many advantages stem from this business for funds are now being used which would previously have been idle, or been put to less profitable use. There is a greater flexibility in the movement and placement of funds which means that the enterprises which need it most are able to get it and quickly – as long as they can pay the price. But there are still some problems to be worked out, for the impact of movements in the Euro-currency markets on domestic monetary policies and on conditions in all domestic short term markets are considerable. Moreover the huge volume of Euro dollars has proved to be a dangerous source of funds for currency speculators. With many international currencies in a far from stable condition the need for some control of the Euro-currency market is evident.

7. GOVERNMENT POLICY

The theory and operation of government economic policy has been examined in some detail in *The Control of the Economy* in this series. This includes an up-to-date assessment of monetary policy including the changes of September 1971. The analysis which follows is more concerned with the ways in which *banks and markets* operate as vehicles and venues for government economic policy and the effect on these institutions of this policy. It is not suggested that the driving force behind most of the activities of these banks and markets is not the profit motive; but perhaps such considerations as the smooth working of the home economy, the part played by the country in the world economy, and the quality of the service to customers, weigh more heavily in this sector than in most.

Traditionally banks and markets have been used by the government to bring about changes in the money supply through the use of such monetary weapons as bank rate, funding, open market operations, quantitative and qualitative directives, and, more recently, special deposits. The Radcliffe Committee (Report on the Working of the Monetary System, 1959) was particularly interested in the effectiveness of these weapons in the management of the economy. Because the aims and exercise of monetary policy are complex and sometimes contradictory, this policy has been only partially effective in use. Only if it is applied with great vigour, which may in itself create a crisis of confidence in the money, will the policy produce prompt and profound effects. For really effective management of the economy a suitable combination of monetary, fiscal and physical measures have to be used, but this is the subject of another book.

A strong connection between the level of demand, and the supply of money has long been argued, and it has been widely accepted that by controlling the supply of money through monetary policy the level of demand can be regulated. But the complicated nature of the monetary system – *the banks and markets* – of this country makes the definition of the make-up of the supply of money a matter of some controversy. Perhaps more useful than the early definition of the money supply as that which is readily available as a means of payment, is the more general concept of 'the whole liquidity position that's relevant to spending decisions' (Radcliffe). It was the *banks and markets* which affect the relative liquidity of potential spenders that most interested Radcliffe in this context, and it was found that these institutions are competing in a single market for credit, so that no one group should be made the exclusive vehicle of monetary policy. Each type of bank and market has its own qualities and characteristics but they are all dealing in credit and even in the 'commodity' is not homogeneous, the market for credit is unified. Forces affecting one group of institutions are likely to have repercussions throughout the market. Even the institutions dealing in the external assets and liabilities (gold, foreign currencies, foreign bonds, etc.) of the country are part of this market system, and the decisions of these international *banks and markets* have a direct influence on the whole liquidity position.

As in any market, the ruling forces of this inter-related system of *banks and markets* are demand and supply, and it is changes in the price of money which is most effective in bringing about changes in these forces. The price of money is the rate of interest, and it is evident that whatever measures the government uses to change the demand and supply of money, it will be those that work through interest rates that will be most effective. Here the government meets with conflicting aims. As manager of the National Debt, the Bank of England, acting for the government, must attempt to keep servicing costs (the amount paid out in interest) to a minimum. As agent of the government's monetary policy the Bank may have to enforce higher interest rates to cut back demand.

The policy of concentrating monetary weapons on the activities of the clearing banks and the discount houses has come in for a great deal of criticism. It is clear that the deposits of the Scottish and Northern Ireland banks, the merchant banks, and the overseas banks provide an important part of the money supply. Indeed, with total sterling deposits at more than £8,000 million in 1971, their deposits are almost as great as those of the clearing banks, and if their foreign currency deposits are included their total deposits are much greater. Moreover, such institutions as building societies, insurance companies, finance houses, investment trusts, and unit trusts, with huge resources at their disposal, are not without a powerful influence on 'the whole liquidity position'. The monetary measures which operate through control of capital issues, clearing bank advances and customer credit must be less effective if the activities of these other financial institutions are not brought under the same control, for if one source of finance is cut off then borrowers will find a source of funds in these other institutions. The success of a lock-gate in holding back the main flow of the stream is greatly reduced if there are channels which are circumfluent of the lock.

It is hoped that this examination of developments in *banks and markets* in the decade since the Radcliffe Report throws some light on several of the questions being asked by students of monetary policy. How do monetary institutions function as vehicles of government policy when that policy is often not obviously in their own interests? Is the policy made more or less effective by the way they operate? Is it reasonable that the policy should work largely through the institutions of the short term money-market? But these questions are to a large extent irrelevant if this examination bears out the Radcliffe view that the money supply does not play a critical role in the economy. Of course the monetary policy may have objectives other than control of the quantity of money, as when it is used to affect exchange rates or in the management of the National Debt.

The Chicago School takes the view that monetary policy has a significant effect on money supply, and that control of this quantity of money plays a critical role in determining the level of activity in the economy. Using data for the years 1881 to 1967 Professor Milton Friedman has shown that there is a close correlation between year to year changes in the quantity of money and those in income (and thus in spending). These changes in money and income cannot be explained as simply the common consequences of another factor, say autonomous investment, for they reflect the stronger and more consistent influence of the money supply. Changes in the quantity of money, after a time lag, have a major impact on changes of output in the short period. In the long period growth is more closely related to changes in prices, that is an increase in the supply of money is followed by a similar increase in prices. So it is in relation to changes in the supply of money that monetary policy to control output and prices can be shown to be most effective. But the actions of the monetary authorities have more often been examined in relation to their effects on *credit*, and this is a less reliable indicator of the impact of monetary policy. This raises again the essential question of how money supply and credit should be defined (see above p. 111) for it is argued that money supply changes at very different rates from the volume of particular types of credit, or total bank credit. The official U.K. definition of money supply includes the total of coins and notes in circulation, the total amount in current and deposit accounts in domestic banks, and the total of deposits at accepting houses, overseas banks and the discount houses, while the Chicago School excludes the latter from their definition of money. The deposits of these institutions are regarded as credit.[1] To complicate the matter further, the 'Letter of Intent' signed by the British Government in negotiating a further loan from the I.M.F. in 1968 introduced a wider definition of money supply.[2] An increase in the money supply was described as *Domestic Credit Expansion* (D.C.E.) and this included the category Public sector borrowing from overseas as well as the three categories already included in the U.K. official definition. In arguing for this additional indicator David Kern[3] said 'since an external surplus is associated with a monetary inflow and an external deficit with an outflow it is clear that the recorded growth in the money supply does not reflect accurately the real rate of monetary expansion'. D.C.E. is a flow concept and Bank of England tables show changes over quarterly periods related to the initial stock of money balances. The items are:

1. Bank lending to the public sector
   (*a*) Central Government
   (*b*) Northern Ireland Government
   (*c*) Local Authorities
   (*d*) Public Corporations
2. Bank lending to private and overseas sectors
   (*a*) Private sector
   (*b*) *less* Foreign currency lending for investment overseas
   (*c*) *plus* Lending in Sterling to non-residents
3. Notes and Coin in circulation with the public (increase)
4. Overseas lending to public sector
   (*a*) Central Government
   (*b*) Local Authorities
   Total = Domestic Credit Expansion

The definition of D.C.E. excludes any form of credit creation which does not lead directly to any change in the money supply, e.g. a transfer of existing money balances from lender to borrower. It excludes any credit created by financial intermediaries outside the

[1] *N.W.B.R.*, November 1969.
[2] *B.E.Q.B.*, September 1969.
[3] David Kern, *N.W.B.R.*, November 1970. 'Implications of D.C.E.'

banks or directly by persons or companies, for example in the form of trade credit. The definition also excludes credit to the private sector from overseas (though such credit will indirectly affect the composition and to some extent the total of D.C.E. because it affects the external transactions of the public sector).

In December 1972 the Bank of England began to present their information on the money stock somewhat differently. The purpose of the rearrangement was to 'indentify more clearly certain areas of interest or influence within which the authorities may operate, and which are liable to affect the total of the money stock'. The rearrangement shows D.C.E. to consist of:

The sum of (*a*) public sector borrowing requirements
(*b*) purchases of public sector debt by the private sector
(*c*) Bank lending to the private sector
plus (*d*) Bank lending in sterling to overseas residents
less (*e*) Bank lending in foreign currencies to U.K. residents for investment abroad

which is consistent with the previous arrangement (see above) but giving different emphasis.

The table below, which comes from *Control of the Economy*, summarizes the main definitions of the money supply.

The argument over what constitutes the money supply is clearly of much more than academic importance. Whether categories are excluded or included, which counts as money and which as credit, is obviously vital to the effectiveness of measures designed to control the money supply and, through that, the level of economic activity. Without the correct information monetary policy may be misdirected. Without control of all the institutions contributing to the money supply a way will be found around the restrictions.

Whether these categories are excluded or included – which counts as money and which count as credit – is obviously vital in any argument over the effectiveness of monetary measures on money supply, and of changes in money supply on the level of economic activity.

Government action designed to restrict the total assets of banks and markets is considered by some economists to have less effect than actions which bring about a change in the structure of these assets.[1] The structure of banks' assets in the distribution of these

[1] *L.B.R.*, October 1969.

Table 33. DEFINITIONS OF THE MONEY SUPPLY

Definition includes	Currency in Circulation	Current Account Deposits	Deposit Account Deposits	Deposits at Accepting Houses, Overseas Bank Discount Market	Public Sector Borrowing from Overseas
Chicago/Monetarist	✓	✓	✓		
Official U.K. M1	✓	✓			
Official U.K. M2°	✓	✓	✓	✓	
Official U.K. M3*	✓	✓	✓	✓	
D.C.E.	✓	✓	✓	✓	✓

* Including all sterling and non-sterling deposits held with U.K. banks by both private and public sectors.
° Both at commercial banks and discount houses.

holdings between liquid and less liquid items in their balance sheets. If banks increase their reserve assets, say by selling bonds in the bond market, they can increase the money supply (their deposits) by up to eight times the amount involved, given a reserve assets ratio of $12\frac{1}{2}$ per cent. If banks can be persuaded to reduce their reserve assets (by buying bonds in the bond market) then the money supply will be contracted. So control of advances is a poor way to control the money supply, the essential prerequisite is control of the monetary base by affecting the flow of reserves in the banks.

The structure of interest rates and their differentials within the money markets were seen by Radcliffe to be at the heart of monetary control. If changes in interest rates persuade banks, institutions, and private investors to hold their assets in a form which takes longer to mature, than in more liquid forms, then the money supply, or at least the velocity of circulation, will have been reduced. Here again the problem of contradictory aims is apparent for such persuasion would involve a rise in long term interest rates which would increase the cost of debt management. Moreover higher interest rates make money more expensive, discourage borrowing and therefore investment, and sap business confidence. The aim of the monetary authorities must be to achieve a balanced growth of the money supply and the level of investment while keeping the general level of prices and the cost of debt management under control, so that the general level of economic activity generates a low level of unemployment, equilibrium in the long term balance of payments, and a satisfactory rise in the standard of living. The limitations of monetary policy as a means to achieve these ends was argued strongly by Radcliffe, but the more recent research of the Chicago School has shown that monetary measures have a vital part to play in the whole strategy of government economic policy.

The apparent lack of effectiveness of the monetary measures used in Britain in recent years to control inflationary pressures has to be explained by those who argue for a purist monetary approach to supplant the present Keynesian approach. They reply that recent 'monetary' measures have operated on credit rather than money and that these measures have been neutralized because the government has permitted the money supply to increase, partly to satisfy the needs of public finance and to maintain orderly conditions in the gilt-edged market. The money supply increased because controls of advances, H.P. restrictions, and higher interest rates were not stringent enough, even with tight fiscal constraints. By allowing the build-up of an excessive supply of money the government's attempts to cut back the level of demand using physical controls has inevitably been less successful than it would have been had the whole monetary base been contracted. However the need for greater flexibility in the movement of interest rates, the rates of unemployment, the level of wages and prices, which is implied in the use of purely monetary policy, made it impossible to accept this as an unmodified alternative to the previous Keynesian approach of government economic policy. With the powerful inflationary build-up of the early 1970s the government resorted to heavy doses of physical measures. At the same time however the Government allowed the new arrangements for control of credit to be given an airing.

COMPETITION AND CREDIT CONTROL, THE NEW ARRANGEMENTS

In May 1971 the Bank of England issued a consultative document outlining for the banks and other financial institutions its proposals for improving the competitive atmosphere and for making its control of credit more effective. The main arguments for the new arrangements have been discussed earlier in the book. The changes were heralded in statements by the Chancellor of the Exchequer, Mr Barber and by the Chairman of the Committee on Consumer Credit, Lord Crowther. In his 1971 budget speech the Chancellor stressed the need for more flexibility in monetary control so that more scope could be allowed for competition and innovation in the banking system. Discussing consumer credit he argued the need for more effective controls of the banking sector and 'other relevant credit giving institutions', particularly the finance houses.

The Crowther Report on consumer credit recommended that there should be but one set of rules on all borrowing and lending, and that the artificial divisions, for control purposes, between bank and non-bank financial institutions should be removed. The controls should be quantitative with a view to the whole money supply, and not selective. Crowther recommended the banks to encourage more personal term loans, and other formal medium term loans. The proposals, as outlined in the consultative paper, make use of some of the ideas outlined by Professor Bain in Appendix 30 of the Report of the Select Committee dealing with the Bank of England. He argued for a system of variable liquidity reserve or ratio requirements. Institutions should be required to deposit cash with the authorities in a ratio to total liabilities subject to variation in the light of official policy decisions, and aimed at the target variable of total private sector lending rather than at the lending of particular institutions.

The chief criticisms of the range of controls existing at time and available to the monetary authorities may be summarized as follows:

(*a*) they were cumbersome and unwieldy,
(*b*) they caused distortions in the money markets,
(*c*) they were ineffective.

Specific complaints came from particular institutions affected by control measures, e.g.:

(*a*) ceilings on lending applied to banks and finance houses stifle competition and are inequitable between lenders, (*b*) the clearing banks have the additional disadvantage of having to keep deposits tied up in cash and liquid assets well above their working needs. Special deposits are a further encumbrance.

(*c*) the threatened cash deposits scheme for financial institutions other than clearing banks and the term controls on consumer lending by the banks restricted competition and initiative.

(*d*) the banks were only able to compete through subsidiaries and through services.

So by the end of 1970 the pattern in the distribution of money and near-money shown in the table below indicates the importance of other institutions as well as the domestic banks. This may have been a distortion brought about by the monetary policy of the authorities and the lack of competition in some parts of the banking sector.

Table 34. DISTRIBUTION OF MONEY AND NEAR MONEY

	%		%
Cash in circulation –	10	Post Office Savings Bank –	5·3
Domestic Banks deposits –	36·9	Finance Houses –	1·6
Building Societies –	30·6	Discount Houses –	0·5
Trustee Savings Bank –	7·7	National Giro –	0·2
Accepting Houses and other banks –	7·2		

Source: *Economist* May 22 1971.

Several reasons are advanced why the share of the domestic banks at the end of 1971 was not as large as it had formerly been:

(*a*) The special limitations (which we have referred to earlier), imposed on the banks by the authorities.

(*b*) The operation by the banks of collective agreements which limit competition.

(*c*) The competition of non-bank financial intermediaries and the high interest rates offered by these institutions.

(*d*) The changes in the means of making payments.

The banks have been responding to increased competition from the P.O. Giro, the Trustee Savings Bank and others by increasing the efficiency of the services they offer and particularly the means of payment. But the introduction of Credit/Access cards, Cash dispensers, Bank Giro and so on has affected the liquidity of the deposits held by the banks. This money is becoming less a liquid asset and more a means of payment. Edward Davis argues that such developments as automatic money dispensers will force deposit taking institutions to become near-money managers offering more attractive rates and undertaking new forms of business. They can no longer take their current accounts for granted.

The introduction of the new arrangements for competition and credit control has done a good deal to modify a situation in which there was little point in the clearing banks going all out to compete for more business when the authorities policy on lending prevented them using extra deposits profitably.

The new deal

The new rules governing competition and credit control came into operation on September 16 1971. They are as summarized below:

1. Freedom for competition for deposits by the banks, and ceilings on lending removed.
2. The cartel arrangement to keep the deposit rate 2 per cent below Bank rate was ended.
3. Overdraft and loan rates no longer linked to Bank rate.
4. Special deposits have been repaid and the banks have been required to subscribe for about £750 million worth of government stock yielding between 5·6 per cent and 6·7 per cent.
5. The banks are required to maintain a ratio of at least 12½ per cent reserve assets to eligible liabilities.
6. Items defined as acceptable by the Bank of England for reserve purposes are:
   a) Cash at the Bank of England, but not in the tills
   b) U.K. Treasury bills
   c) Money at call in the London money market. [Originally money at call in the Inter bank market was not acceptable but by January 1973 money lent at call to jobbers on the London Stock Exchange and that lent to certain money brokers was regarded as eligible for reserve assets if secured against gilt-edged securities.]
   d) Government Bonds with less than one year to run to maturity
   e) Local Authority Bills eligible for discount at the Bank of England
   f) Commercial bills eligible for rediscount at the Bank of England but only up to a maximum of 2 per cent of eligible liabilities.
7. Eligible liabilities are defined as:
   a) the deposits in sterling of the banking system as a whole with a maturity of less than two years

b) any sterling obtained by switching from foreign currencies
c) Inter bank transactions and sterling certificates of deposit (on a net basis).

8. Merchant banks and British overseas banks must hold 12 per cent of their assets in a liquid form, and finance houses with assets of more than £5 million must keep 10 per cent.
9. Finance houses may apply for bank status.
10. The Bank of England may call on banks and finance houses for special deposits. The Scottish banks will be favourably treated in the percentage called. A differential rate as between domestic and overseas deposits might be applied. An additional or separate rate of call might be applied to each bank's liabilities to overseas residents in sterling or in foreign currencies.
11. Discount Houses were at first required to maintain a 50 per cent minimum public sector lending ratio but this was modified in July 1973 (see p. 75). The syndicated bid for Treasury bills was abandoned. They are also affected by the replacement of Bank rate by the 'last resort' minimum lending rate.
12. As from January 1973 clearing banks were allowed to hold a stake of more than 25 per cent in acceptance houses.

Further changes of importance to the way in which credit control affects the business of *banks and markets* were announced about the same time as the above measures were coming into effect. The authorities declared that 'the Bank will no longer be prepared to respond to requests to buy stock outright, except in the case of stocks with one year or less to run to maturity; they reserve the right to make outright purchases of stock with more than a year to run solely at their discretion and initiative.' So the 'open back door' by which the Bank had acted as 'lender of last resort' is no longer unrestricted, and the *Economist* argued the failure of this aspect of the Bank's credit control operations had been recognized.

Next, there was a change in the functioning of Bank rate. Many authorities had been for some time questioning the effectiveness of Bank rate changes in bringing about changes in monetary demand. The new arrangements further reduced the significance of Bank rate as a major influence on all other rates for money and, in particular, the lending and deposit rates of the clearing banks. However the function of Bank rate as the minimum at which the Bank would normally lend to the discount market remained, and it was considered important that the rate for this function should be able to respond flexibly to changing conditions in the money market without the implied heralding of shifts in monetary policy which attended changes in Bank rate. The new rate, known as 'Bank of England's minimum lending rate to the market' became operative on October 13 1972 and is fixed by the formula: '½ per cent above the average discount rate for Treasury bills established at the weekly tender rounded to the nearest ¼ per cent above.' The rate normally becomes effective, for lending by the Bank, from the following Monday. It is still open to the Bank to manipulate the minimum lending rate to signify a shift in monetary policy just as previously Bank rate changes had done this. The intention behind the new arrangements is clearly that control should operate through interest rates but the authorities have reserved the right to interfere with the free working of market rates.

Short-term effects of the new arrangements

There has been a dramatic increase in the money supply (though this is not to suggest that the rise is due to the new arrangements alone). In M3 terms the money stock grew from around £15,000 million early in 1968 to around £19,000 million at the end of the third quarter of 1971, when the new arrangements began to come into force. Since that date the rate of increase has stepped up considerably. In the following twelve months it increased by £5,000 million to £24,000 million (approximately) and the rate only slightly declined in 1973. The narrower definition of money stock, M1, increased much more slowly.

Table 35. MONEY SUPPLY

£m.

End of 1st Quarter	M^1	M^3	Financial Year	D.C.E. £m
1968	8190	14900		
1969	8480	16010		
1970	8620	16350	1969/70	– 651
1971	9810	18370	1970/71	+1064
1972	11230	21160	1971/72	+2358
1973	12430	27300	1972/73	+6945
1974	12772	34210	1973/74	+7821
1975	14890	37770	1974/75	+6382
1976	17960	40850	1975/76	+5138
1977	19750	44920	1976/77	+4933
1978	24300	51100	1977/78	+3769
			1978/79	+7314

Source: *B.E.Q.B.*

Before we examine the part played by the banks, under the new arrangements, in this monetary expansion, two further causes of this dramatic increase should be outlined. Firstly the need to foster economic expansion, in fact a rate of growth not previously successfully maintained, produced a marked reluctance on the part of the government to restrict the rate of monetary expansion. *The Times* in commenting on the lack of balance between the rate of economic growth and the rate of growth of the money supply argued 'The overriding monetary objective should remain a rate of growth in the money supply no greater than the desired rate of growth in the economy as a whole at current prices. That would involve halving the annual rate of expansion in M3 . . .' Secondly the rapid monetary expansion coincided with a high official borrowing requirement as the government account moved back into deficit. Nor will the 'neutral' budget for 1973–74 have changed this position substantially. Unless a government is successful in selling debt to the public at large the banks' deposit base will be increased and from this base there will be an expansion in bank lending.

The bank's part in the expansion of the money supply stems partly from the change from a liquidity ratio requirement of 28 per cent to a reserve assets ratio requirement of 12½ per cent, and partly from the removal of the quantitative controls on lending and the repayment of Special Deposits. The banks have thus been free to expand their advances and since new advances create new deposits the banks lending policy has helped the money supply to expand. In the event the banks were not left completely unrestricted in their expansion of advances. Because of the way that eligible reserve assets and eligible liabilities have been defined the assets freed were a good deal less than a straight comparison of the 28 per cent and 12½ per cent ratio might suggest. 'Reserve assets' is a narrower definition than the previous 'liquid assets', and 'eligible liabilities' wider than 'deposits'. Banks were, right at the outset of the new arrangements, required to subscribe for £750 million worth of government stock which soaked up a good part of their 'freed' assets. Then although Special Deposits were repaid to the banks in September 1971, the growth of the money supply in 1972 provoked a new call in November of that year and a further call a month later, making in all 3 per cent the result of which was a total of more than £700 million being deposited with the Bank. The Authorities obviously considered that the rapid rise in house and land prices in 1972 was partly due to increased bank lending for the Bank issued a directive that lending to property speculators should be less readily available.

The government, with the goal of a high rate of growth uppermost, has demonstrated its reluctance to apply the brake for fear of a return of all the problems associated with a 'Stop-Go' policy. The only real concession made early in 1973 to those clamouring for a slowing down of the 'headlong pace of expansion' and to the need to adjust the Payments position, which at that time was running at a rate of deficit consistent with an annual figure of about £800 million, was to reduce the level of government expenditure planned for that year, and to plan for a reduced rate of growth for the following year. In terms of monetary policy affecting *banks and markets* there was greater freedom than had been enjoyed for many years. The few measures designed to restrict advances seemed to hold few real problems for other banks. They found a way round measures aimed at their reserve assets and bond holdings by heavy borrowing in the inter bank market and by use of sterling certificates of deposit. These relatively liquid but non-eligible items provide the banks with a highly flexible buffer to the authorities' attempts to control credit. The main attempts of government economic policy were at that time however centred on controlling consumer demand by a policy of physical controls – a prices and incomes freeze.[1]

From this short term analysis of the effects of the new arrangements on control of credit through the *banks and markets* we must turn to the effects on competition between these various institutions. The growing competition between the banks and other institutions has been a constantly recurring theme of this book. Before the new arrangements the banks had claimed that they were unfairly hampered in their attempts to compete widely in the markets for money, and to a large extent they relied on their subsidiaries to carry out this competition for them. This pattern is already changing. Banks are beginning to compete more directly in areas of medium and even longer term finance, and competition for deposits, without which any continued expansion of advances is impossible, has become increasingly fierce. Midland Bank led a consortium which successfully bid for Thos. Cook. National Westminster and Barclays sold off minority holdings in finance companies presumably to give themselves more freedom to compete directly with those institutions. Lloyds Bank has bought out all the outstanding shareholders of one

[1] See *Control of the Economy* by D. Lee in this series.

of its finance house subsidiaries, and also produced a scheme to provide reciprocal credit facilities for customers in conjunction with banks in Germany and France. Midland Bank announced a similar scheme which also extended to the United States. Several banks launched or developed insurance services. The proposed merger between two merchant banks Hill Samuel and Slater Walker, the former an acceptance house, would have created the largest merchant bank in the U.K. But all of this activity offers little in the way of major new departures from traditional banking business, and amounts to little more than marginal adjustments to their interests.

Perhaps the most significant development has been in bank lending. There was no sudden and dramatic expansion with the removal of controls in September 1971, but a gradual increase based largely on the growth of consumer expenditure: personal lending then expanded rapidly. Industrial investment was slow to respond to the new impetus but as manufacturing industry began to expand the Bank directed that this growth should be sustained if necessary at the expense of the property speculators who had been among the first to take advantage of the easement of controls on bank lending. Throughout 1972 the personal sector continued to borrow heavily from the banks and to a lesser extent from finance houses. Financial Institutions other than banks increased their financial liabilities by 3 per cent more than in 1971. This is, of course, the increase in the funds available for their use. The table below shows the source of the increasing funds of these institutions compared with that of the clearing banks. It is on the basis of these increased liabilities that

Table 36. CHANGES IN THE LIABILITIES OF FINANCIAL INSTITUTIONS IN 1972 (£m)

	Increase in Deposits	*Increase in Total Liabilities*
Clearing Banks	+ 4804	+ 5408
Building Societies	+ 2193	+ 2190
Savings Banks	+ 356	+ 356
Investment and Unit Trusts	+ 241	+ 663
Finance Houses	+ 34	+ 205
Insurance Companies Pension Funds and Property Unit Trusts	—	+ 2450
Others	—	+ 684

these institutions have been able to increase their lending. The finance houses have complied with the requirement that they should keep a 10 per cent reserve assets ratio. The ratio had reached 10·1 per cent by September 1972 and was at 10·5 per cent in May 1973. For a brief time in March 1973 it had been at 13·4 per cent. The clearing banks have adapted their assets to the new requirements. This has not been a particularly painful process for them as it has generally meant an increase in the funds available for advances. By November 1971 the reserve ratio was 15·3 per cent; a year later and after the call for Special Deposits it was 14·2 per cent, and in May 1973 14·6 per cent. The clearing banks obviously hoped to maintain their reserve assets sufficiently above the 12½ per cent minimum requirements to give themselves room for manoeuvre in the event of a more restrictive monetary policy. However in August 1973 Lloyds were the first bank to take rapid steps to restore a reserve assets ratio which had fallen below the minimum requirement.

A comparison of Table 36 with Table 34 suggests that the banks have been able to hold their own with these other institutions in the competition for funds. This competition has undoubtedly been one of the factors responsible for the rapid rise in interest rates. The government, anxious that the money supply should not expand too rapidly, has generally been prepared to allow the rates to go on rising. There was some indication early in 1973 of a levelling out of rates but in later months the continued rise in interest rates caused a good deal of concern. Building society lending rates reached an unprecedented 11 per cent and even this rate was not considered high enough to allow a sufficiently attractive rate to be offered to

Table 37. CHANGES IN INTEREST RATES

Last Working Days	*March 1971*	*March 1972*	*March 1973*
Bank rate or minimum lending rate	7·00	5·00	8·50
Treasury bills	6·67	4·33	8·06
Clearing banks' base rate	9·00	4·50	9·50
Finance houses' base rate	—	5·50	11·00
Clearing banks' deposit rate	5·00	2·50	7·50
Local Authority temporary loans	7·50	4·94	10·13
Euro dollar and deposits in London	5·38	5·53	8·69
National Savings	5·74	5·74	5·74

'investors'. Government interference on behalf of the societies was forthcoming, and in November 1973 minimum lending rate was raised to a record 13 per cent. Table 37 shows how interest rates changed between March 1971 and March 1973.

The new arrangements have brought about some changes in *banks and markets* in the short term. The next chapter will examine the longer-term developments of Competition and Credit Control (C.C.C.). However, there was already some support for the statement made by Edward Davies that 'to the extent that banks can substitute their lending for that of other intermediaries they will need to consider diversification of their asset structure and conversely a wider range of deposit liabilities' after only two years. The effectiveness of the new arrangements for control of credit was more severely tested by a number of critical pressures in the years 1973 to 1976.

8.
RECENT DEVELOPMENTS IN BRITISH BANKING

The banking sector has seen many significant developments in the 1970s, some of which were merely a continuation of those which were already evident in the previous decade and some which evolved from pressures which were manifested for the first time in this decade. The pressures bringing about the changes have come both from inside and outside the British Economy. New institutions have grown up and the Authorities have attempted to produce new controls to deal with these new institutions and the new situations they have helped to create.

We have seen in earlier chapters that the banking sector includes:

London Clearing Banks
Scottish Clearing Banks
Northern Ireland Banking
Accepting Houses
Other British Banks
and Overseas Banks, including
American and Japanese banks

It also includes consortium banks, which are those owned by other banks. No single bank owns more than 50 per cent of their capital, and at least one of the participating banks will be an overseas bank. The banking department of the Bank of England, the Discount Market and the National Giro are also important elements of the Banking sector. All the offices of the banks which observe the uniform reserve assets ratio introduced in the Competition and Credit Control measures of 1971 are thus accounted for.

The importance of the banking sector to the economy as a whole in this decade is most clearly understood when we consider the contribution it makes in providing the funds which fuel economic activity. Without these funds in 1978 agriculture and fishing would have been more than £1,250 million worse off, mining and quarrying £1,300 million, construction £1,600 million, manufacturing industry £9,000 million, the Service Industries (including transport, retail distribution;

professional and scientific services) £12,000 million. Moreover, other financial institutions would have been looking for some £7,000 million and private individuals would have had to find another source for £4,500 million. This reinforces the point that it is the function of these banks to meet the needs of all sectors without putting at risk the funds left with them for safe keeping. In his presidential address to the Institute Bankers in 1977, C. J. Montgomery picked out six major areas in which the Clearing Banks were developing their commercial banking services to other sectors of the economy while continuing to observe the essential principles of banking. These areas of development were in:

(*a*) Consumer Credit
(*b*) Finance for Industry and Commerce
(*c*) Sterling and currency markets
(*d*) Money transmission
(*e*) Advisory services
(*f*) Other financial services

Consumer credit

We have observed in earlier chapters the developments which had occurred in recent decades: the introduction of personal loan schemes in the 1950s for example, was an attempt not only to improve the range of services to personal customers but also to engage in an area of profitable lending after a long period of credit restraint. Such schemes also enabled the clearing banks to compete more effectively with the Hire Purchase companies which had dominated consumer credit up to that time. The removal of restrictions in 1958 enabled the clearing banks to take equity holdings in these Hire Purchase companies and even to take them over completely. Flexibility in providing consumer credit was maintained by making available short term facilities either through the more traditional type of loan account linked to base rate or through overdraft facilities. In the 1960s Credit Cards first came to the UK from America. Barclaycard was introduced in 1966 and Access followed in 1972. All banks now provide revolving credit to customers and non-customers alike and international links established during the 1970s enable card holders to use other cards in most parts of the world. No doubt in the future we shall see further steps along the path to the advent of the 'Cashless Society' but we have some way to go before even the most sophisticated computers will enable us to settle all our debts by means of personal card payments.

Finance for industry and commerce

There is no doubt that a new spirit of competition in the world of commercial banking is producing profound changes in their market behaviour. However, the banks are not without their critics in this area of the development of banking services to industry and commerce. The primary role of the banks, according to Mr Montgomery, is the provision of short term finance to cover working capital requirements. However, the need for the banks to be involved in providing longer term funds, particularly for smaller businesses, was advocated as long ago as 1931, by the Macmillan Committee. The banks responded by setting up, and supplying capital for, the Industrial and Commercial Finance Corporation. Its object was to meet the apparently unfulfilled demand for funds by smaller businesses – to close the so-called 'Macmillan gap'. A further step in this direction was taken in 1961 when the Authorities agreed to allow the guarantee of the Export Credits' Guarantee Department to be used to back medium term lending. In 1973 clearing bank interests in providing long term finance were expanded when the Industrial and Commercial Finance Ltd., and the Finance Corporation for Industry Ltd., merged under a new parent Finance for Industry Ltd. In company with the Bank of England and the Scottish Banks, the Clearing Banks not only subscribed further capital but also made available substantial stand-by facilities to this Company.

We have observed earlier that there are other ways in which the banks assist in the business of supplying medium or even long term capital to industry. These include *leasing* facilities, first introduced in the 1960s, which removed the burden of capital outlay from smaller companies. Under these schemes banks purchased capital items – factories, major processing plants, ships, aircraft, oilrigs and a wide range of plant and equipment were made available in this *factoring* process. However, it is in this sphere of medium and long term lending that the need for funds to be offered at attractive rates of interest is still evident. The banks argue that 30 per cent of their lending is already in this category and although they recognize that term lending is here to stay they consider that a substantial increase in the present proportion would attend against prudent lending principles. Bankers clearly understand their role in an economic system in which the inter-dependence of the industrial and banking sectors has existed for a long time. 'It is inconceivable that society at large, whatever be the form of Government reflecting that society, would permit the banking system to retain the role of holding a substantial part of the shorter term savings of the nation without, at the same time, meeting the proper requirements of Industry,' concluded the Cambridge Banking Seminar. The stresses and strains appear however at the point where industry, deprived of any realistic alternatives, looks to the banking system for funds which can only be supplied with danger to the liquidity of the banking system. Inherent dangers would be magnified if banks were to increase their holdings of industrial equities. The problem remains how best to contribute usefully to the efficiency of industrial enterprise without neglecting its existing responsibilities.

From the chart showing the sources and uses of funds for industrial and commercial companies it is clear that although external funds emanating largely from the Banks continued to increase from 1970 to 1973, in 1974 and 1975 there was a reduction in those funds. Even in 1976, when this source again increased, it did not match the increase in internal funds which now account for a higher proportion than at any time in the last decade.

As a result of the concern of the Government and small businesses over the shortage of funds for industry, the Wilson Committee was established in 1976 to investigate this shortage and to look into the workings of various financial institutions. These institutions have been invited to give evidence and it has emerged that there is no unanimity in support of the view that small businesses are in reality short of funds. The Confederation of British Industry argued that expected *profitability* is the vital question: firms will not and should not invest if the resultant profitability is inadequate. But profitability depends heavily on the *rate of interest* being charged for borrowed funds and these are partly determined by inflationary pressures and by external forces (e.g. the need to prevent the outflow of funds to other countries). Undoubtedly, industrial investment has been hindered by high interest rates. However, the *Midland Bank Review* (August 1976), pointed out that industry is hardly likely to invest to expand *capacity* when there is already plenty of spare capacity available. The public sector can also be criticized for attracting an unduly large proportion of the Banks' funds although after 1977 the borrowing requirement was somewhat lower than earlier in the decade. Inability to sell gilt-edged stock at certain times led to the syphoning of private non-Bank liquidity into treasury bills. Companies having surplus funds in advance of their investment spending requirements, were encouraged by the treasury bill rate to place their money in this way rather than reduce their Bank borrowing. This

SOURCES OF FUNDS OF ALL INDUSTRIAL AND COMMERCIAL COMPANIES

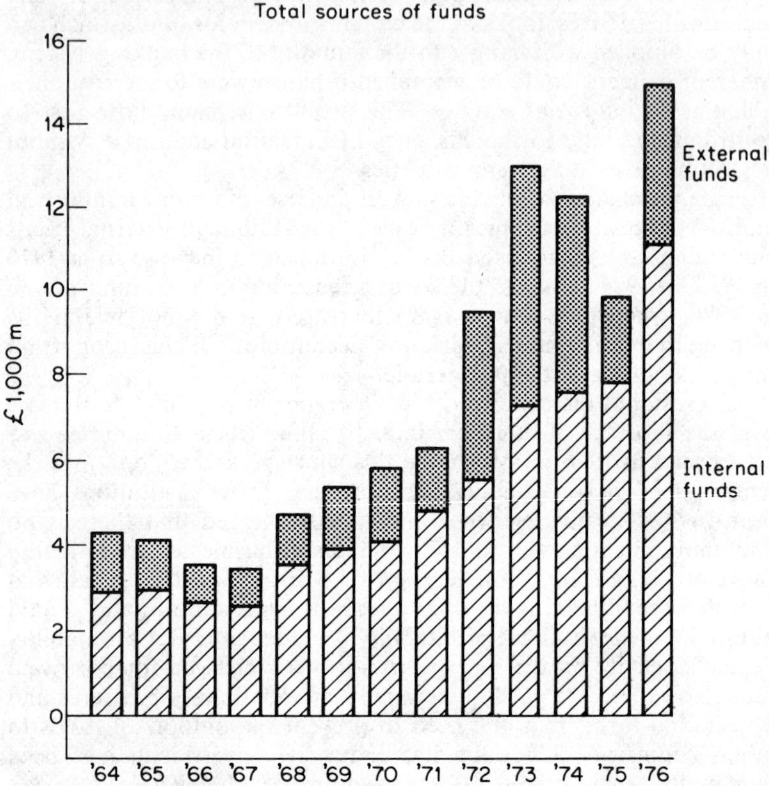

Source: Economic Progress Report (Treasury Information Division), December 1977

ties up funds which could otherwise be made available to smaller firms.

The Banks are, therefore, by no means the only institutions under criticism. The huge *Pension Funds* have responded in the later 1970s by becoming much more involved in the provision of *risk* capital. Institutions, like the National Coal Board Pension Fund, have established units specifically to assess the investment possibilities of enterprises requiring *venture* capital. These Pension Funds have become a major force in the City and they have ever broadening links with other financial institutions including the Banks and especially the Merchant Banks, with whom they are co-operating in a number of investment projects. This, in line with the recommendations of the *Bolton Committee* which reported in 1971 that 'There should be a variety of sources of finance, institutional or otherwise, for budding or expanding businesses to approach so that survival is not put at risk by sheer absence of financial facilities'. It also concluded that the health of the small business sector required a taxation system which would enable individuals to acquire or establish new businesses out of personal resources and to develop them on the basis of retained profits.

Nationalization

Criticisms of the Clearing Banks came to a head in the demand particularly by left wing economists for the *nationalization of the banking system*. They argue that if the banks were nationalized their funds would be at the disposal of the government which could then ensure that they reached those industries which needed finance. Other critics looked enviously at the very large profits made by clearing banks in the later 1970s and suggested uses to which they could be put. It is recognized that banking costs could be cut if the present wasteful duplication of resources could be eliminated. Protagonists of nationalization say this will only be achieved under the direction of a national banking corporation, so that in place of the four or five High Street Banks, side by side, there would be just one branch of the nationalized bank. Moreover, deposited funds could be used more selectively and would not be exploited by property, or other, speculators. The Government's control of the money supply would be much more effectively carried out through this institution which would be directly under the control of the Treasury.

Although the clearing banks mounted an effective campaign against nationalization, there remains a case for a State clearing bank to provide further competition for the Clearers. Such banks exist in France and Italy. One proposal for establishing a State commercial bank suggested this could be achieved by merging the National Giro with the National Savings Bank for this purpose. There are however many difficulties, for banks are not built in a day and with several well established powerful competitors there would be all the problems of breaking into a well organized oligopolistic market. The infrastructure of banking is very complex and the economics of scale are very large. It takes years to build the base of deposits and loans on which successful banking is dependent.

Two reasons given for the demand to establish a State clearing bank are the need for more effective competition to the Big Four than that currently provided by the Co-operative Bank and the Trustee Savings Bank. Secondly, current provisions by the State – the Giro and then the N.S.B. – have only limited efficacy. Merging them would make sense, for they both operate through the Post Office and their services are complementary – the N.S.B. collecting deposits and the Giro providing a money transmission service. Up to now the Giro has not achieved the same success as its parallels in Holland and West Germany in earning a significant share of the market. There is no suggestion that the market is already saturated by present banking facilities for more than 40 per cent of all adults still have no bank account. The list of Banking Deposits below shows that the Big Four have by far the largest share of existing deposits. However the N.S.B. has a considerable deposit base at present entirely invested in public sector eligible stock.

BANKING DEPOSITS, 1977 (£m)

The Big Four	£9000
N.S.B.	£2000
Giro	200
T.S.B.	18

Although the Trustee Savings Bank has a small deposit base it has begun the process of lending out traditional deposits. Initiatives of this sort are clearly needed by the N.S.B. for, during the 1970s when money incomes have doubled, its deposits have stagnated.

While a merger with the Giro could help there are difficulties. Getting two management teams to work together would be a problem. There could be intolerable pressures on the present Post Office organization for although there are 22,000 offices, which are open for longer hours than the clearing banks, it is currently hard stretched to maintain the present level of its services. Moreover, making banking loans requires a great deal of expertise and good managers do not come easily or cheaply. Thus, while the clearing banks may have fought off the current demands for nationalization, and the problems associated with the setting up of a state clearing bank are many, these are issues which are likely to come to the fore again in the 1980s.

Public control of bank lending

The banks have long recognized the right of the Authorities to ensure that banks are lending in the public interest. The problem is how to identify and apply this interest. We have seen that the Bank of England has a wide variety of powers which it can use to exercise control. Thus while the banks have been criticized from time to time for the quantity and direction of their lending there is no denying that the powers have been available to the Authorities to exercise greater control over this lending had they so wished. An examination of the use which the Authorities have made of these controls during this decade and the changes they have made in them would illustrate this point.

Earlier chapters have shown that prior to the introduction of the Competition and Credit Control measures in 1971, a system existed which had been built over a long period and which had been modified in part by the findings of the Radcliffe Committee. They had commended policies designed to influence the cost or availability of credit flows to various sectors as the means of overall control. Monetary policy, operating through interest rates, was, to them, the proper method of affecting financial conditions and through them, the level of demand and this was, they considered, 'an instrument of singular potency'. However, distortions were caused by this system of credit control during the 1960s and the arbitrary and damaging impact of hire purchase controls on particular industries. Circumstances demanded more severe restraint than could be achieved by acting through cash or liquidity ratios so direct controls and the imposition of lending ceilings appeared to be essential. However, we have seen that ceilings on lending related to each bank's position on some arbitrary date and truly stifled competition. Competition had been further limited by collective agreement or cartel arrangements between clearing banks not to compete on interest rates paid on deposits and charged on advances.

These quantitative limits on banks' advances to private sector borrowers prevented efficient banks from expanding more than inefficient ones and favoured established customers more than up and coming ones. The growth of fringe banks set up to get round these quantitative restrictions occurred because the ceilings applied mainly to the clearing banks. In Chapter 7 we described how pressures for the reform of this system of control produced the Competition and Credit Control Measures. Ceilings on bank advances and H.P. controls were removed and control through liquidity ratios was replaced by control through the ratio of reserve assets to eligible liabilities. Moreover, these reserve assets ratios were applied uniformly across the whole banking system, and Bank Rate was replaced in 1972 by the Minimum Lending Rate.

Prior to 1971, the Authorities were able to limit the banks' ability to make advances by keeping down their own borrowing or borrowing more from the general public through National Savings or using a longer term debt not recognized as liquid assets. Open Market Operations could be used to force the banks to call in loans from other money market institutions; but the system lacked effectiveness because the Bank of England would always help these institutions over liquidity troubles, by buying their holdings of gilt edged stock to steady the market and keep down the cost of financing the National Debt.

The Bank of England still retains more general control over the direction of lending through qualitative lending guidance, the so-called 'moral-suasion'. The Governor of the Bank writes to all relevant banking institutions asking them to give priority to certain borrowers and to restrict lending to others. Guidance of this kind has almost always been followed by the banks. *Midland Bank Review* (August 1976) describes the use of 'moral-suasion' when a number of secondary banks got into financial difficulties in 1973 through investing liquid funds in illiquid assets including property advances. Mr Healey referred to this as a major crisis in banking history. The Bank of England recognized its responsibility for the security of the banking system but it did not want to be directly involved in the scheme to save the funds of depositors. Instead, it instigated the 'life-boat scheme' under which the major banks, predominantly the clearing banks, were presumed to be recipients of the short term deposits withdrawn from the secondary banks and agreed to recycle these funds back to the banks concerned so as to give them time to put their affairs into better order. The clearing banks experienced some losses by giving this support for it took some time for the system to recover from the tremors caused by this crisis.

The effectiveness of C.C.C.

These are by no means the only shocks and pressures which the banking system has had to weather since the introduction of C.C.C. The purpose of these measures was to regulate the supply of credit through the market mechanism in the context of a more competitive banking system and, at the same time, to give the authorities more effective control over the banking system as a whole by bringing within its scope the non-clearing banks, which had been expanding rapidly under comparatively light control. When C.C.C. was introduced the level of economic activity was such that an expansion of bank credit was considered likely to be helpful in stimulating recovery. The consequent rapid increase in the money supply from 1972 to 1974 was accentuated by the distortion of statistics by the new definitions introduced in C.C.C. M3 was distorted by arbitrage operations on a vast scale. When the banks needed greater liquidity they could sell certificates of deposit, and use the proceeds to buy reserve assets. It was cheaper to sell C.D.s bearing high interest rates to obtain the last little bit of liquidity needed to meet reserve ratio requirements than to raise base rates which would put up the cost of borrowing on all deposits. However this created a merry-go-round or arbitrage operation for companies found that when C.D. or other wholesale deposit rates went above base rates, they could borrow from the banks on overdraft to lend back on C.D.s thus making a safe profit. In this way both bank advances and bank deposits were increased leaving the banks' liquidity situation worse than before. This rise in deposits inflated M3 without adding any real increase to company liquidity.

Such episodes in banking experience have been used to criticize the failure of the banks to operate in the public interest but it is argued in the *Midland Bank Review* that, at any time during this period, had they wished to control bank credit more tightly the Authorities had adequate means available to them. The money supply was allowed to grow because of the government's wish to increase the level of economic activity at a time when unemployment was rising rapidly and industrialists were showing a marked reluctance to step up fixed investment. What is more the Government needed the co-operation of the T.U.C. in restraining wage demands.

Although the Authorities and the banking system weathered the storm caused by the collapse of the secondary banks a whole range of other factors combined to force the Authorities to slam on the brakes. This contributed to the financial crisis, the collapse of the stock market and the continued rapid rise in unemployment. We have explained that the secondary banks collapsed when the property speculation bubble burst. Those fringe banks were overlent on property as speculators had borrowed from that at 14 per cent to buy properties whose rental income might yield 4 per cent. They gambled on inflationary pressures pushing up rents and prices so that capital gains would take care of things. However, supply had been over expanded, interest rates rose, rents were frozen and property prices tumbled. Other factors contributing to the financial uncertainty in the mid-1970s included the miners' strike and the three day week, the wage explosion and the price freeze, the cost of holding stocks when commodity prices exploded, and they combined to put company profits under strain, bringing many famous companies and their bankers into trouble. Stock prices tumbled particularly when interest rates on liquid assets yielded more than equities.

Despite all these pressures the Authorities did not return to quantitative controls or ceilings on advances except in the introduction of 'The Corset' – a supplementary deposit scheme penalizing banks whose interest bearing deposits rose over a specified rate. Banks have found the operation of the Corset increasingly irksome, for it has restricted this ability to profitably take advantage of the slow recovery in investment confidence in the later 1970s.

Policy instruments

So the C.C.C. measures have survived a period of intense pressure and the powers and methods of control appear to be adequate. If the system is not working in the public interest, critics should specify its inadequacies before any changes are made. The Wilson Committee may supply these criticisms. The Bank of England claims that its policy is not necessarily conditioned by the economic and institutional circumstances currently in existence. Its approach is pragmatic and now gives much more attention to the growth of money supply than in the previous decades when a more rigorous Keynesianism dominated its policy. We have seen that monetary weapons are among the standard policy instruments available to the Authorities. However, they have difficulty in realizing their policy aims with any precision while using these instruments. Some economists (see Prest: *Manual of Applied Economics*) doubt whether the Authorities have the necessary knowledge about the relationships between instruments and aims. The problem of defining the degree of manipulation needed to achieve a specific objective is even more difficult in an open economy like that of the U.K. which is heavily dependent on external trade and which may, for instance, find its ability to affect interest rates or the reserve base severely restricted by conditions in the money markets in the rest of the world. Prest argues that 'Optimal policy in a world of uncertainty and incomplete knowledge poses extremely difficult questions'.

Competition

What of the new atmosphere of competition which C.C.C. was to have ushered in? There is no more evidence now of direct price competition between the clearing banks although they have operated for very short periods on marginally different base rates. There is more competition in wholesale money with variations in the banks' tenders for bigger business deals and more competition through banking services and bank charges. The Price Commission which investigated bank charges in 1978 advised the banks not to subsidise bank charges. These should reflect the time costs. On the other hand interest should be paid on all deposits including current accounts. The combined losses of the four Clearers on their money transmission service of £664 million in 1977 is offset by the interest rate benefit enjoyed on these accounts. The Commission also wanted to see the streamlining of the branch banking system with the elimination of duplicated units. Barclays have been discussing with the Union of Bank Employees the redundancies which will follow the reduction in the number of branches. They failed to obtain Union agreement to a return to Saturday opening linked to a staff productivity deal. Since Saturday closing they have lost a great deal of profitable business to the Building Societies. The Clearing Banks consider that they have suffered from the 'unfair conditions' under which they compete with the Building Societies. The advantages of tax relief given to depositors with Building Societies enable them to offer interest rates which are more attractive to tax payers than those of the Clearing Banks. In evidence to the Wilson Committee, the Clearers pointed out that their share of the deposit market has declined from 45 per cent in 1962 to just over 30 per cent in 1976 while in the same period Building Societies increased their share from 20 per cent to nearly 40 per cent. They now have assets of more than £30 billion. The Building Society movement has been strengthened by a series of mergers: thirteen in 1976 and eighteen in 1977. As an example, the merger of the Anglia with the Hastings and Thanet made it number fourteen in the league table of Building Societies with assets of more than £1·2 billion. The increased scale of their business has enabled them to substantially increase their High Street representation with more than 3600 branches in 1977 compared with about 1000 branches in 1967. Competition for the Clearing Banks in money transmission would be intensified if the Building Societies joined the clearing house system and this is under active consideration. The Trustee Savings Bank is stepping up its attack in that part of the market (the 40 per cent without a bank account), where the Clearers must look for their future current account growth. So, while competition between the Big Four is not apparently much increased, there are other institutions offering effective competitive facilities.

The American Banks

Competition is coming not only from domestic institutions, for foreign banks are increasingly making their presence felt. The Chairman of the American Banks' Association of London in 1978, reviewed the development of the American banking presence. He described phases in this development, of which the first covered the period from 1892 to 1930, when large U.S. commercial banks, predominantly from New York, established branches in the City to service the requirements of the U.S. companies in the U.K. and to provide finance for international trade. The second phase was associated with the growth of the Euro dollar market which was described in Chapter 6. The remaining large and many medium size U.S. banks arrived and, while continuing their previous activities, the American Banks expanded into a much wider range of international business. This included medium term finance for a range of international companies, and Euro-dollar lending to Governments and international projects, usually on a syndicated basis. The third phase, from 1968, saw the arrival of additional U.S. banks and growing activity by U.S. banks in the sterling markets, following the introduction of C.C.C. in 1971. In response to the greater demand for competition in lending, U.S. banks began to develop and sell more specialized services. In 1978 there were fifty-seven American banks directly represented in London and, if we include indirect representation through London based consortia banks, the number of American banks with interests in London has gone up considerably in the last decade. Four main features emerge from an analysis of the American presence in London:

1. American banks continue to be major participants in Euro currency market; nearly 90 per cent of their deposits are in currencies other than sterling and these banks account for over one-third of all foreign currency liabilities of banks in the U.K.

2. The most important part of their business is international and nearly two-thirds of all their assets consist of currency lent to overseas residents.

3. American banks account for 15 per cent of the total market in advances to U.K. residents, including public and private sectors.

Table 38. BANK DEPOSITS

Mid-year Currency (£m)	*American* (£)	*American* (*Frgn*)	*London Clearing* (£)	*London Clearing* (*Frgn*)	*Accepting Houses* (£)	*Accepting Houses* (*Frgn*)	*Other Overseas* (£)	*Other Overseas* (*Frgn*)
1974	4121	25080	22060	2920	2089	2737	542	8962
1975	4158	32781	22566	3983	2255	2775	2404	18344
1976	4608	38835	23705	4655	2623	3233	2767	24140
1977	5612	45096	25095	5171	2973	3534	3258	30307
1978	6671	44188	30136	6021	3435	3989	4614	35408

Source: *BEQB*

Most of this lending is to medium and large corporate borrowers and to Government agencies. These banks have a special interest in North Sea Oil development. Other advances are made to finance exports and imports in the short term and to finance investment, trade and business development in the long term.

4. Their sterling lending has grown steadily. U.S. banks now account for nearly 10 per cent of all sterling advances to U.K. residents.

American banks are attracted to the City of London for many reasons. Their Chairman mentioned five in his address:

(*a*) Communications with the rest of the world by telephone, mail and electronic device are the best of any country in Europe. The common language of the two countries re-inforces this advantage.

(*b*) The cost of doing business in London is comparable to that of any other major European centre.

(*c*) Britain has a large pool of educated capable professional and salaried workers.

(*d*) The City has preserved a genuinely open attitude towards competition, change and innovation.

(*e*) Within the small area of the City there is a tremendous range and diversity of expertise. The American banks are certainly providing a spur to competition and the major British banks must look to their laurels if they are to meet this growing challenge as well as that from other foreign banks.

The Merchant Banks

The Merchant Banks are equally feeling the cold wind of competition. The most significant feature of their history has been their flexibility and their ability to adapt to the changing conditions and the requirements of their clients and customers. This ability is being seriously tested in the 1970s. John Paddon, Chief Executive of County Bank has summarized merchant bank business as corporate financial advice, the taking of deposits and sterling and currency money market operations; foreign exchange dealings, medium term lending and the syndication of loans; acceptance credits and all forms of export finance; the holding and dealing in quoted and unquoted investments; and fund management on behalf of their clients, most typically pension funds, unit trusts, investment trusts and wealthy individuals. A noticeable trend in the later 1970s has been the emergence of merchant banking subsidiaries of the powerful clearing bank group in serious competition with the more traditional operators. Established Merchant Bank houses have been bought up by the Clearers: e.g. Samuel Montague by Midland; County by National Westminster; others have developed strong links with foreign or overseas banks.

The powerful pressures on the banking system have been no less important in their effects on the Merchant Banks. The combination of high inflation with recession, the weakness and fluctuation of sterling coinciding with high interest rates and the decline in sterling's role as a reserve currency and as an investment medium would have required the best of the traditional adaptability of the Merchant Banks. Add to this the explosion in commodity prices, particularly oil, and the emergence of new nations, notably in the Middle East as world wide investors and providers of funds, and all the economic and financial consequences of our entry into the Common Market, the massive investment in North Sea Oil development and the rise and fall of the value of real property and you have a set of circumstances of such turbulence that many financial institutions, and the Merchant Banks included, suffered such a buffeting that they will never be the same again. They claim their position has not been improved by government policy which was founded on massive public expenditure requiring its own funding, a surfeit of statutory regulation on matters ranging from taxation to price, wage and dividend restraint and a further shift in the balance of power in favour of the Unions. All this, while bringing home strongly, even to the smaller companies, the need for more competitive trading abroad.

Critics, including Ronald Pullen of *The Times*, argue that the Merchant Banks have responded too defensively to the challenge of unstable economic circumstances coupled with competition 'muscling in from all directions'. Others predict the eventual eclipse of the Merchants as they are absorbed into Universal Banks along the lines of their European counterparts. But the Merchants have 'a chameleon like instinct for altering the thrust of their business as circumstances change'. In the 1950s we have seen that they moved into corporate finance work; in the 1960s they exploited the wholesale money markets and in the 1970s they are developing the possibilities of the Euro-currency and international Bond markets. In the 1980s, Pullen expects them to forge more links with large overseas banks and generally to expand the international scope of their business.

The Merchant Banks have their weaknesses. The years of inflation and the effects of sterling depreciation have seriously damaged their balance sheet ratios – three-fifths of their deposits are in overseas currencies. Because of their wish to retain family control, some of the houses have been unable to look to rights issues to improve the capital base. They have been forced to look for outside links e.g. Warburgs have turned to France. But there is a limit to this form of co-operation if control of activities is to be retained within the U.K. The growth of competition in the traditional fields of business of the Merchant Banks is further cause for the deep rooted concern about their survival as independent institutions, particularly when the limitations of their size restricts their ability to compete with the foreign and overseas banks in London which have huge deposit bases and branch networks. Perhaps even more significant has been the Clearers' desire to gain access to the wholesale money markets to compensate for the sluggish growth of retail deposits. By supplementing overdraft with medium term finance the Clearers have come into more direct competition with the Merchants whose forte has long been setting up medium term lending syndicates and arranging acceptance credits. While the Merchant Banks will have to extend

Table 39. ACCEPTING HOUSES' PERCENTAGE SHARE OF BANKING SECTOR

	Total banking liabilities	*Sterling deposits*	*Eligible liabilities*	*Reserve assets*
1974	4·5	4·9	3·8	3·9
1976	4·1	5·4	4·5	5·3
1978	4·1	5·6	3·8	4·0

Source: *BEQB*

their relationship with other financial institutions to provide them with access to bigger capital resources, the whole British banking system will have to direct its attention towards increasing its capacity to meet the international challenge if it is to maintain its traditional primary position in the world's money markets.

BIBLIOGRAPHY

BOOKS

Main Texts

Balogh, T., *Studies in Financial Organization*

Clarke, William M., *The City in the World Economy*

Dacey, W. M., *The British Banking Mechanism*

Einzig, P., *Textbook on Monetary Policy*

Ferris, Paul, *The City*

H.M.S.O., *Pamphlet No.* 24

Macmillan Report, The, *Report of the Committee on Finance and Industry*

Pringle, R., *Banking in Britain*

Radcliffe Report, The, *Report of the Committee on the Working of the Monetary System*

Samuelson, P., *Economics*, Chapters 16 & 17 (for U.S. System)

Sayers, R. S. *Modern Banking*

Wadsworth, J. E., *The Banks and the Monetary System in the U.K.* 1959–1971

Government policy and the money market

Einzig, P., *Monetary Policy: Ends and Means*

Friedman and Schwartz, *A monetary history of the United States* 1867–1960

Johnson, H. (ed), *Monetary Policy in Britain* 1959–1969

Newlyn, W. T., *Theory of Money*

Bank of England

Clapham, J., *The Bank of England*

Institute of Bankers, *The Bank of England Today*

Report of the Select Committee of the House of Commons on the Nationalised Industries. Sub-Committee on the Bank of England

Clearing banks

The London Clearing Banks: *Evidence by the Committee of London Clearing Bankers to the Committee to Review the Functioning of Financial Institutions*

BANKS AND MARKETS

Nevin E, and Davies, E. W., *The London Clearing Banks*

The Report of the Monopolies Commission on the proposed merger of Barclays, Lloyds and Martins Banks

Revell, J. R. S., *Changes in British banking – Hill Samuel Occasional Paper No.* 3

Sayers, R. S., *Lloyds Bank in the History of English Banking*

Discount market

Allen, Harvey and Ross, *This is bill broking*

Gillette Bros., *The Bill on London*

Institute of Bankers, *The London Discount Market Today*

King, W. T. C., *A History of the London Discount Market*

Scammell, W. M., *The London Discount Market*

Merchant banks and the capital market

Henderson, R. F., *The New Issue Market*

Kellett, R., *The Merchant Banking Arena*

Macrae, N., *The London Capital Market*

Morgan, E. V. and Thomas, W. A., *The Stock Exchange – Its History and Functions*

Young, George K., *Merchant Banking, Practice and Prospects*

The new markets

Einzig, P., *The Euro-Dollar System*

Martenson, G. C., *The Euro-Dollar Market*

Glendenning, A. B., *The Euro-Dollar Market*

ARTICLES

Monetary policy and the money markets

'The Management of Money day by day' *BEQB March 1963*

Newlyn, W. T., 'The Supply of Money and its Control' *EJ June 1964*

Crouch, R. L., 'The Inadequacy of New Orthodox Methods of Monetary Control' *EJ December 1964*

Cramp, A. B. 'Control of the Money Supply' *EJ June 1966*

'Money Supply and the Banks' *MBR February 1969*

'Domestic Credit Expansion' *BEQB September 1969*

'The Control of Bank Deposits' *LBR October 1969*

'The Control of Bank Deposits' *NWBR November 1969*

'The Importance of Money' *BEQB June 1970*
'The Stock of Money' *BEQB September 1970*
'Another Look at Money Supply' *MBR November 1970*

Bank of England
'The Work of the Branches' *BEQB December 1963*
'The note circulation' *BEQB March 1965*
'Official Transactions in the Gilt Edged Market' *BEQB June 1966*
'A Short History of Exchange Control' *BEQB September 1967*
'Bank Regulations in Britain – By "Suasion" not Statute' *MBR November 1967*
'The Bank's Overseas Work' *BEQB December 1967*
'The Bank of England as Registrar' *BEQB September 1968*
'The Exchange Equalisation Account' *BEQB December 1968*
'Managing the Gilt Edged Market' *MBR May 1969*
'The functions and organisation of the Bank of England' *BEQB May 1975*
'The work of the Cashier's Department' *BEQB September 1970*

Clearing banks
'The Bank Mergers', L. Baragwanath, *BM Vol. CCV*
'Monetary Policy and the Mergers', Davies & Nevin, *BM Vol. CCV*
'The Branch Problem' *The Banker Vol. 118–1968*
'The Twilight of Banking', G. Norman *BM September 1969*
'Towards an Effective Liquidity Ratio?' *MBR May 1970*
See also the Annual Reports of the Clearing Banks

Discount houses
'The London Money Markets – Long term trends reviewed' *MBR May 1966*
'The London Discount Market: some historical notes' *BEQB June 1967*
'Recent Developments in London's Money Markets I. The Clearing Banks and the Discount Houses' *MBR August 1969*

Merchant banks – the gold market and the capital market
'International Capital Markets of Europe' *BEQB September 1970*
'Precious Metals' (insert) – *BBR November 1970*

The new markets
'London's New Markets for Money' *MBR August 1966*

BANKS AND MARKETS

'Recent Developments in London's Money Markets II. Continued Expansion in "Complimentary" Markets' *MBR November 1969*
'The Euro currency business of banks in London' *BEQB March 1970*
'The Euro currency business of banks in London – maturity analysis as at end of July 1970' *BEQB December 1970*
'Eurodollars – Economic Progress Report' *HMSO January 1971*
'Eurodollars – Economic Progress Report' *BM February 1971*
'Eurodollars – Economic Progress Report' *BM March 1971*

See also the Annual Review of Banking in *The Times, Financial Times* and *Economist*, and various publications of The Institute of Bankers.

BEQB	Bank of England Quarterly Bulletin
EJ	Economic Journal
MBR	Midland Bank Review
LBR	Lloyds Bank Review
BBR	Barclays Bank Review
BM	Bankers' Magazine
NWBR	National Westminster Bank Review

OTHER ARTICLES

'Banking Regulation and Competition' *MBR November 1971*
'The Gilt Edged Market and Credit Control' *MBR August 1971*
'The Operation of Monetary Policy since the Radcliffe Report' *BEQB December 1969*
'The Financial Institutions' *BEQB December 1970*
'International Finance and the Euro Dollar Market' *NWBR November 1971*
'Banking enters a New Era' *MBR May 1972*
'Monetary Policy and CCC' *NWBR November 1972*
'The Implications of DCE' *NWBR November 1970*
'The Strains of Monetary Expansion' *MBR May 1973*
'Does the money supply really matter' *BEQB June 1973*
'Papers submitted to the Wilson Committee' *BEQB September 1978*
'International co-operation in banking supervision' *BEQB September 1977*
'Public control of bank lending' *MBQ August 1976*
'London Clearing Banks' evidence to the Wilson Committee' *NWBR May 1978*

ESSAY QUESTIONS

1. What is Bank Rate? Who fixes it? What effect does it have on the commercial banks? (JMB).
2. Distinguish between the functions of the Bank of England and those of the Joint Stock Banks. (JMB).
3. How does the Bank of England control the granting of credit by the commercial banks. (JMB).
4. 'Advances create Deposits'. Explain.
5. In the light of experience since 1955, consider the effectiveness of regulating the British economy through the banking system.
6. What is the 'liquid assets ratio' of British clearing banks? What is its significance?
7. The New York money market has no exact equivalent of the London discount market, and yet works a monetary system very similar to ours in other respects. Suppose our discount houses went out of business: how could their essential functions be performed by the existing institutions in the city. (O. & C.)
8. Are mergers of major commercial banks likely to have any significant effect upon the operation of monetary policy in Britain. (O. & C.)
9. Explain the meaning of the following terms used in the banking business (*a*) Bank overdraft (*b*) Crossed cheques (*c*) Night safe (*d*) Deposit account (*e*) The Bank Rate. (JMB).
10. Discuss the part played by the discount market in the British monetary and banking system. (WJB).
11. A bank buys long term securities from a bank depositor. What, if anything, happens to (*a*) bank deposits, (*b*) the bank's reserves, (*c*) the bank's reserve ratios?
12. Discuss the respective functions of joint stock clearing banks and merchant banks. Is there any need for their separate existence? (O. & C.)
13. How can the banking system help to promote economic growth? (AEB).
14. What are Treasury Bills? Explain their importance in the London money market. (AEB).
15. Discuss the effects of growing competition on the banks and institutions of the money markets.

16. The Radcliffe report said there was a single market for credit. Is this still true?
17. How does a commercial bank make its profits? (JMB).
18. Describe the operations of the London money market and discuss their significance in the British economy. (R.S.A. Intermediate).
19. Describe the structure and workings of the London New Issue Market.
20. Do banks create money? (O. & C.)
21. 'Money was tight in the money market yesterday; some institutions were forced to borrow small amounts at bank rate. The squeeze on bank advances will apparently continue.' (*The Times*, financial report). Explain and discuss. (O. & C.)
22. 'During periods of credit restriction, profits of joint stock banks are squeezed and their chairman feel quite free to criticize government economic policy; yet by their actions, the banks make this policy more effective.' Explain and discuss with reference to post war experience. (O. & C.)
23. Would you advise British Joint Stock Banks to adopt the continental practice of providing long term finance for industry (Cambridge Scholarship).
24. What influence does the Bank of England exert through its position as 'lender of last resort.' (Cambridge Scholarship).
25. Is the capital market efficient? (JMB).
26. What explanation would you offer for the recent mergers in British Industry. (JMB).
27. How is long term capital obtained (*a*) by new firms (*b*) by firms already established? (JMB).
28. Discuss the advantages and disadvantages of the main methods which may be used in a poor country to obtain finance for investment.
29. Outline the main means by which a company can obtain funds to finance expansion, and consider their relative merits.
30. Suppose that the Government borrows an additional £200m. by issuing Treasury Bills to that amount in order to finance its current expenditure. Trace the likely effects that this would have on the supply of money.
31. Is it important for the authorities to control the quantity of money? (Oxford Scholarship).
32. Do banks create money? (O. & C.)
33. Assume that, as a result of the next budget, the U.K. Government's budget deficit will be substantially reduced. Analyse the

expected effect on the growth of output, on the volume of bank deposits, and on the price level – (O. & C.)

34. Banks have recently been asked by the Government to restrain the rate of increase in their lending to 5 per cent a year. What would happen to output and the level of prices if they expanded their loans twice as fast? (O. & C.)
35. Is there a relationship between the volume of bank deposits and the level of prices? (O. & C.)
36. Should an investor who firmly expects Bank Rate to fall sharply in the very near future buy long term bonds or sell them? Briefly indicate why.
37. What effect does an open market purchase of securities by the Bank of England have on the commercial banks in the U.K.?
38. How may the banks contribute towards the maintenance of a high and stable level of employment? (WJB).
39. From what sources do firms raise money to finance their activities? What factors determine which sources a firm uses? (London)
40. What effect is the Bank of England's new set of rules for competition and credit control likely to have on the structure of banks and markets?

For Multiple Choice Questions on this topic see Chapter 7 of *Objective Tests in Advanced Level Economics* by Vivian Anthony and Donnan Baron (Heinemann).

Chapter 13 in Vivian Anthony's *Objective Tests in Introductory Economics*

Chapter 8 in G. F. Stanlake's *Objective Tests in Economics.*

Chapter 12 in E. Nevin's *A Workbook of Economic Analysis.*

The reader should not expect to find the material for the answers to all these questions in this book. They are given as a guide to the sort of questions which are being set by examiners in the whole field of money and banking. However the book should be helpful in providing some part of the material needed for a good answer to many questions set out above.

The subjects covered by the book are partly descriptive, and partly applied economics, and because the theory is only included when it seemed to be essential for an understanding of the text, the reader is advised to work on obtaining a thorough understanding of the theory from one of the standard texts before attempting many of these questions.

INDEX

Acceptances, 77
Accepting houses, 15, 43, 45, 47, 101, 123, 132, 145–7
Accepting Houses Committee, 22, 69, 77
Agriculture, 132
American Banks, 132, 144–5
Assets, eligible reserve. *See* Reserve assets

Banks
- American, 27, 43, 45, 51, 85
- British Overseas, 43, 85
- Clearing, ix, 9, 86. *See also* Commercial Banks
- Foreign, 45
- Scottish, 30, 36

Bank advances, 39
Bank of England chapters 1 and 7, 132, 139, 140, 142
- Balance sheet, 5
- Banking Department, 7
- Branches of, 17
  - and Clearing Banks, 10
- Departments of, 17
- Directives of, 12
- Discount market, in the, 15, 61
- Domestic role of, 4
- Issue Department, 6
- Moral suasion, 13
- Private customers of, 16
- Profits and efficiency of, 19
- Public accountability of, 18

Bank Rate, 15, 30, 53, 103. *See also* Minimum lending rate
Barclays Bank, 29, 45, 50, 52, 55, 82, 87, 128, 143
'Big Four', 29, 50
Bolton Committee, 137
Building societies, 49, 123, 129, 143

Cash deposits, 22
Cash ratio, 10, 31
Certificates of Deposit, 38, 62, 70, 99, 141
Chicago School, 117, 120, 121
Clearing banks, chapter 8
Commercial banks, chapter 2
- Advances, 39
- Deposits of, 28, 43
- Investments of, 37
- Mergers, 29, 48, 55
- Profits, 54
- Recent developments in, 42
- Services, 41

Commercial bills, 67–72, 124
- Discount rates of, 33, 69
- Resurgence of, 71
- in the Clearing Banks, 33

Competition and credit control, 115, 122–31, 132, 139–44
Computers, 51
Consortium banks, 132
Construction industry, 132
Consumer credit, 133
'Corset', 142
Credit cards, 122, 133
Credit controls, 56
Crowther Report on Consumer Credit, 122

Discount houses, 15, chapter 3, 123, 125, 132
- Assets of, 72
- Usefulness of, 66

Discount market, chapter 3
Borrowing in, 59
Lending in, 62
Source of funds, 60
Domestic Credit Expansion, 118–20

Eligible liabilities, 124
Euro-currency markets, ix, 46, 89, 99, 105, 130, 144
Euro-dollars, 24, 45, 107, 109
Exchange Control, 2
Exchange Equalization Account, 3, 7, 19
Export Credit Guarantee Department, 134

Fiduciary issue, 6
Finance houses, x, 22, 49, 99, 125
Foreign banks, 145, 146, 147. *See also* Banks, American
Friedman, Milton, 117
Funding, 16

Giro, national, 123, 132, 137
Gold, chapter 5
Gold hoarding, 93
'Good' money, 60
Government bonds, 8, 16, 38, 73

Hire purchase companies, 133
Hire purchase controls, 22

Industrial and Commercial Finance Corporation, 134
Industry, finance for, 134–7
Inter-bank market. *See* Secondary money markets
Insurance Companies, 49
International Monetary Fund, 4
Issuing Houses Committee, 76, 78

Keynes, 121, 143

Leasing, 134
Lender of last resort, 12, 14
Liabilities, eligible, 124, 147
Liquidity ratio, 10, 34
Lloyds Bank, 29, 30, 45, 52, 55, 128, 130
Local authorities market. *See* Secondary money markets
London Discount Market Association, 15, 59
London gold market, 3, chapter 5
Members of, 92, 97
Recent developments in, 94
Working of, 91

Macmillan Committee, 134
Manufacturing industry, 132
Merchant banks, x. *See* chapter 4, 125, 137, 145–8
Competition, 84
Financial advisers, role as, 74
International links of, 81
Investment management by, 80
Profits of, 88
Midland Bank, 29, 45, 52, 55, 57, 128, 129, 146
Minimum lending rate, 56, 125–6, 140
Mining industry, 132
Monetary policy, viii, chapter 7, 20–6
Efficacy of, 25
Money supply, 117, 126–31, 141
Monopolies Commission Report on Bank Mergers, viii, 48, 55
Moral Suasion, 140. *See also* Bank of England

National Debt, management of, 9, 61, 112
Nationalization of banks, 137–8
National Savings Bank, 123, 129, 137, 138
National Westminster Bank, 29, 47, 50, 55, 128, 146
New Issues, 78
North Sea Oil, 145, 146

Open market operations, 9, 11, 115, 140

Pension funds, 129, 136–7, 146
Price Commission, 143
Prices and Income Board Report (1966), 53
'Privilege' money, 32, 60
Public deposits, 8

Quarrying industry, 132

Radcliffe Committee Report (1959), viii, 1, 18, 21, 23, 25, 55, 59, 74, 115–17, 120, 121, 139
Reimbursement credits, 77
Reserve assets, 10, 34, 124–6, 130, 147

Secondary banks, crisis, 140–2
Secondary money markets, chapter 6
  Factors contributing to growth of, 102
Select Committee on Nationalized Industries, Report of, viii, 1, 7, 19
Service industries, 132–3
Special and supplementary deposits, 10, 13, 36, 56, 115, 123, 125, 127, 130, 142
Special Drawing Rights, 96

Trade bills, 33, 62
Treasury bills, 1, 3, 13, 33, 58, 63, 104, 124–6, 135
  Discount rates of, 33
  'Tap' bills, 64
  'Market' bills, 64
Treasury, 1, 19, 110
Trustee Savings Bank, 123, 138, 143

Union of Bank Employees, 143
Unit Trusts, 49
Universal Banks, 147

Ways and Means advances, 8
Williams Deacon's, 50
Wilson Committee, 135, 142, 143